The Drummond Books No. 1

AN ACCOUNT OF
FIVE AERIAL VOYAGES
IN SCOTLAND

THE DRUMMOND BOOKS

are published by the Friends of Edinburgh University Library exclusively for their members. This first book is limited to four hundred numbered copies and twenty lettered copies.

This copy is
no. 31

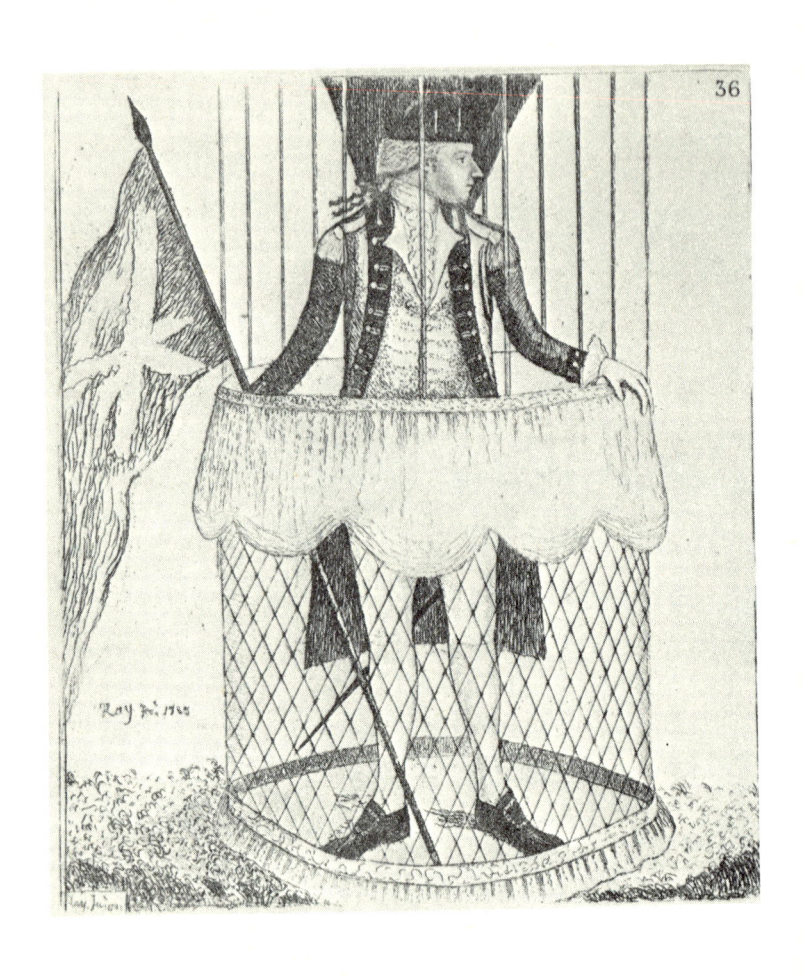

Lunardi, from John Kay's *Portraits*

AN ACCOUNT OF FIVE AERIAL VOYAGES IN SCOTLAND

VINCENT LUNARDI

With an Introduction by Alexander Law

EDINBURGH
1976

This book is published by the Friends of Edinburgh University Library for its members and has been printed for them by Lewis Reprints Limited, Tonbridge

ISBN 0 905152 00 X.

Introduction copyright © 1976 by Alexander Law

INTRODUCTION

The *Caledonian Mercury* of 17th September, 1785 carried the following announcement:—

'GRAND AIR BALLOON. Mr. Lunardi, Secretary to the Neapolitan Ambassador, and the First Aerial Traveller in England, has the honour to acquaint the nobility, gentry, and public in general of Edinburgh and its environs, that he intends gratifying their curiosity with an aerial excursion. As Mr. Lunardi is not induced to make this excursion from pecuniary motives, he wishes only to be insured, that his necessary charges shall be defrayed. It is therefore proposed to open a subscription; and he begs leave to inform the public, that so soon as a sum sufficient to defray the expence is subscribed for, Mr. L. will fix the day of his ascension and will give due notice of the time and place in the public newspapers. Subscription papers are left at the following places. Mr. Creech, Mr. Balfour ... booksellers ... and at Mr. Lunardi's lodgings, in Walker's Hotel, No. 4 Princes Street. Where may be seen different prints of Mr. Lunardi's aerial voyages; also an account of his first and second voyages at Liverpool.'

Vincent Lunardi had arrived in Edinburgh on 12th September, 1785, fresh from successful ascents at London and Liverpool. One of his technical advisers in London was Dr. George Fordyce, a graduate in medicine of Edinburgh University who had a high reputation as a specialist in London, where he also lectured in chemistry and physics: it seems a fair deduction that Fordyce urged Lunardi to visit Edinburgh, a centre of interest in scientific and intellectual matters.

Lunardi was born at Lucca in 1759. On his father's death, his mother was left with Vincent and his two sisters, and the family was helped by a relation, the Cavaliere Gherado Compagni, who held a post in the Court of the King of Naples. Compagni, the 'Guardian' of Lunardi's correspondence, introduced the young man to the Neapolitan service and he joined the Engineer Corps, and travelled extensively in Europe, eventually becoming Personal Private Secretary to Prince Caramanico, Neapolitan Ambassador to the Court of St. James's. It was in 1783 in London that he saw a newspaper account of the feat of the brothers Montgolfier in launching a hot-air balloon at Versailles on 19th September, with a cock, a duck, and a sheep on board. Later that same year J. F. Pilâtre de Rozier, with the Marquis d'Erlandes as his companion, made a flight of $5\frac{1}{2}$ miles with a similar balloon, and on 1st December, the brothers Robert, with the advice of Professor Charles, experimented successfully with a hydrogen-filled balloon. The craze for ballooning had begun, and there was much talk in London and elsewhere of the advantages and disadvantages of Montgolfières and Charlières. With Fordyce's help, Lunardi constructed a balloon and devised equipment for producing hydrogen, and, on 13th September, 1784, in the presence of the Prince of Wales and a large crowd at Artillery Fields in London, he rose successfully accompanied by a pigeon, a dog, and a cat. The pigeon, not unnaturally, escaped: the cat, suffering from cold, was landed when the balloon came down in Hertfordshire, but Lunardi and the dog resumed their flight and came to rest at Standon, near Ware, to the astonishment of the peasantry. Lunardi became a national hero, was presented at court, and made an Honorary Member of the Artillery Company.

Lunardi was the first 'aerial traveller' in England, but he was not the first in the United Kingdom. That honour belongs to James Tytler, who rose in a hot-air balloon from Comely Gardens, near Holyrood and was carried half a mile on the road to Restalrig on 27th August, 1784. This brilliant but unfortunate man, described later by Burns as 'a poor devil in a skylight hat and hardly a shoe to his feet', never received credit for his achievements. His own account of his ascents and the misfortunes that attended them is given in the footnote on page 107. The Edinburgh mob laughed at him, and the *literati* denigrated his attempts somewhat in the style of Alister Campbell's comment on Tytler's unsuccessful second attempt, that his balloon 'rose over a dyke and then quietly settled on a midden'. Lunardi met Tytler in Walker's Hotel: we have no record of their conversation, but the Italian writes kindly of his predecessor on the last page of his book.

The ascents Lunardi describes in this book were five – two from Edinburgh, two from Glasgow, and one from Kelso, and the many reports he quotes from local newspapers testify to the popular excitement. He was a superb showman. The scene of the first ascent, from Heriot's Hospital Gardens comes vividly to mind – the two large cisterns of water covering iron, the vessels with sulphuric acid, the lead pipes attached to the decorated balloon, the bands, the flags flying, the gun sounding from the Castle, the intrepid adventurer himself in a colourful uniform, waving his flag from his basket, or blowing his trumpet. He was particularly lucky in having a striking first ascent: the text of Kay's *Edinburgh Portraits* says, 'All the other ascents since his time have been dosing, sluggish-looking exhibitions, whereas Lunardi went off in the grandest style, precisely resembling a sky-rocket.' There is something very touching too about the accounts of his reception in country places where he landed. There was the Rev. Mr. Arnot of Ceres 'who, with forty or fifty people, came running quite out of breath', or that old man near Glorat who said, 'I have seen Marr's year, and the Highlandmen's Raid, and about twelve years syne, I gaed o'er by yonder (pointing to the Canal) to see ships sailing thro' dry land; but the like of this I never saw. Dinna ye think the world will soon be at an end ?'. In its rhythm and its historical purview, this speech might have been written by Scott himself for one of his characters. There is also the episode of the voice in the Border hills calling out, 'Lunardi, come down'. Mrs. Durham of Largo wrote an amusing account of that first landing near Ceres: 'He flew 8 miles to a place called Craighall, when he called to some reapers throw a speaking-trumpet, who, taking it for the last trumpet, or the divell come in person to carry them away, ran off and left the balloon in a sort of floating undulating state, surrounded by a number of crows, of which that neighbourhood abounds. About a mile further a stout and adventurous farmer, who had read the newspapers, catched hold of the rope and anchor, and with some difficulty fixed it, and relieved our poor adventurer from his carr ... he eagerly kiss'd this good farmer and his assistants ... What surpriz'd and terrified the villagers was that the poultry, and in particular the ducks, all made a noise, and seemed to be conscious of surprize'.

His last Scottish ascent is not described in this book. It took place on 28th July, 1786, when he rose from Heriot's in his 'New Balloon, which is decorated with his Majesty's and the Prince of Wales's arms', and 'is twice as large as the former one'. This may have been the 'transparent balloon' which, under Lunardi's direction, the girls of the Merchant Maiden Hospital constructed for him, which was on view in Parliament House, admission 6d. (*Courant,* 26th December, 1785). He had intended to take Mrs. Lamash, an actress in the Theatre-Royal, with him, but at the last moment decided that his balloon could not support two, and went alone. He came down near Musselburgh, was entertained by Sir William Dick at Prestonfield House, and returned to Henry Erskine's house when, 'As the balloon had still a pretty strong ascending power Mr. Lunardi chose to make his entry into George's Square seated in his triumphal car, the balloon floating in the air a considerable distance above it'. (*Courant,* July, 1786).

Lunardi's Scottish flights were his greatest successes. Later attempts in England were not successful, and perhaps the glamour had worn off. He eventually returned to Italy in April, 1788, after five years absence. We know relatively little of his later life, except that he gave displays in Italy, Spain, and Portugal. The last we hear of him is the notice, during the war, in the *Gentleman's Magazine:* 'July 31, 1806. Died, in the convent of Barbadinos at Lisbon, of a decline, Mr. Vincent Lunardi, the celebrated aeronaut'.

Publicist, adventurer, man of courage as well as conceit, Vincent Lunardi is an attractive figure. The ladies loved him, and the Lunardi bonnets became the height of fashion, 'constructed of gauze or thin muslin ... the upper part expanding into the dimensions of a miniature balloon. He expected the ladies to approve of him, and the only disappointment in that respect that he records is the 'female Machiavel of fifty' who upset his scheme to bring a crowd into George Square to witness his first ascent. We who note the list of aristocratic and legal families then living in the Square, and recall the formidable characters of the Edinburgh ladies described by Cockburn, are perhaps not so surprised. People crowded to see him: it is said that 80,000 watched his first Edinburgh ascent and 20,000 the last ascent in 1786. He always declared he was not in the business to make money but only wished to clear expenses: this is probably true, for he gained what meant more to him the friendship and approbation of the great. He became a freeman of St. Andrews, Edinburgh, and Kelso, an honarary member of the Company of St. Andrews Golfers (ancestor of the Royal and Ancient), of the Royal Company of Archers, of the Cape Club (Glasgow branch), of the Beggars' Bennison of Anstruther, and of the Crochallan Fencibles, of Edinburgh. He was a friend of the famous and witty Henry Erskine, the Dean of Faculty. Lunardi in his gay uniform strikes a theatrical note in eighteenth century Scotland, and his letters provide a fascinating sidelight on the country and in particular on the Edinburgh of the time.

Alexander Law.

LIST OF SUBSCRIBERS

H. M. Adam
James C. Allan, B.A.
Allan, Jean M.
James Maxwell Alston
The Rev. A. Graeme Auld
E. James Baird
Right Honourable Lord Balerno
Professor James Barr
Judith E. R. Barton
Professor William Beattie
Dr. C. A. Beevers
David Bell, M.B.E., MA., B.Com.
Miss M. D. Bell
Marion M. Bennett
Jonquil Bevan
Rev. A. P. Bogie, M.A., F.S.A.Scot.
N. Egerton Browne
W. Norman Brown
Andrew Bruce
Professor H. A. Brück
Geoffrey Bullough
D. L. Bulow
Ian Campbell
Mary G. Campbell
Mrs. J. Menzies Campbell
Dr. Jack Cormack
Alfred T. Cowie
W. N. Craig
Isobel B. Craighead
Professor David Daiches
Fiona Darbyshire
R. A. McL. Davidson
A. C. Davis, O.St.J., M.A.
The Rev. Dr. Walter Bruce Davis, M.B.E.
Stephanie B. Deans, M.A.
Mrs. Andrena M. Dobbin
Professor Gordon Donaldson
Mrs. E. M. L. Douglas, M.A. (Cantab.)
Phyllis M. Downie
Dr. J. J. Drever
H. J. R. Dunn
The Honourable Lord Dunpark
Kulgin D. Duval
The Lord Erskine of Rerrick, G.B.E., K.St.J., D.L., J.P., LL.D., F.R.S.(E), Hon. F.R.C.P.(E).
J. G. Farquhar
George A. Ferguson
Dr. I. S. Ferguson
Professor K. J. Fielding
E. R. S. Fifoot
M. H. Finlayson
Dr. A. Russell Forrest
Alastair Fowler
Dr. Andrew G. Fraser
J. I. S. Gallacher, B.Sc., A.C.A.
Scott I. Galt, LL.B.
Mrs. C. M. Gilruth
J. Hardie Glover
Karl Gollub-Darley
Dr. A. A. Gordon
Mrs. G. M. R. Graham
Douglas Grant
John Grant
Nils Erik Grönn
Ivor Guild
Jean R. Guild
Colin H. Hamilton
Miss C. Hargreaves, B.Sc.
Hannah Harkins
Mrs. H. D. Harrison
Denys Hay
Sir Malcolm Henderson
The Rev. A. C. Hill, C.B.
P. G. C. Hudson
Mrs. Merritt Y. Hughes
J. B. Hume
Miss Ann Hyde
Miss R. Jackson
George L. Jobson, W.S.
Elizabeth Johnston
Miss M. I. Johnston
T. L. Johnston
C. J. Kay
Miss M. E. Kerr
Right Honourable Lord Kilbrandon
Margaret A. Kirkley, M.B., Ch.B.

Dr. James Kirk
Ronald A. Knox
Frederick F. Kortlucke, Jr., M.D.
Alexander Law, O.B.E., Ph.D.
Mrs. James S. Learmont, M.A.
Dr. Thos. W. Lees
Gwyneth Llewellyn, M.A., M.Sc.
J. W. L. Lonie
Rev. T. Waterton Lund
Ronald J. Lyall
Ivan M. Lyon, M.B.E.
The Rev. Geo. I. L. McCaskill
A. M. McCosh
A. Grant McCulloch
Dr. Robert McCurdy
J. A. MacDonald, M.A., M.B., Ch.B.
Peter McDonald
Mrs. Iain MacIvor
Fiona V. MacKelvie
Dr. Neil Maclean
Mrs. Jean M. MacPherson, M.A., Ph.D.
Mary Bruce McWhirter, M.A., B.Sc.
Dr. C. Ogilvie Marr
Mr. L. A. Martin
Linda J. Maxwell
Mrs. J. C. G. Mercer
The Very Rev'd A. Pierce Middleton, Ph.D.
Helen L. G. Miedema
Amy Milligan (Mrs.)
Iain G. Mitchell, LL.B.(Hons.) F.S.A.Scot.
Jeanne R. Mitchell
George & Madeleine Monies
Dr. Audrey B. Morrison
Professor Stuart L. Morrison
Mrs. Norah Napiontek, M.A., M.Litt.
National Library of Scotland
Douglas C. Neillands
Mrs. Mary Nicholson
Miss M. Anne Noble
Sir Charles Normand
Sheila Ann Ogilvie

A. E. G. Pilliner, B.Sc., Ph.D.
John Valdimir Price
J. D. Ralston
David Ramage
Ian M. Robertson
Alistair Rowan
Mary W. W. Sandercock
Rosemary Sansome
George Shepperson
Dr. Ann Silver
Daniel Simpson
R. J. G. Sinclair
A. Skowron, M.D.
Mary Stein Smeaton
Alastair L. Smith
W. Watson Smith
William A. Spence
Alan Stark
Mrs. A. P. Stewart
Mrs. Mary S. Stewart
M. F. Strachan
Lord Stratheden and Campbell
Margaret A. J. Swinley
H. P. Tait, M.D., F.R.C.P.Edin., D.P.H.
Sir George Taylor
D. Ainslie Thin
Roberta S. R. Thomson, M.A.
S. T. Treen
Dr. Agnes F. Turner
Vassar College Library
I. A. Waldie
W. M. Walker
Winifred H. S. Wallace
Charles D. Waterston
(Miss) Elizabeth Watt
John A. Watt
Alford T. Welch
Marion R. West
Elizabeth R. White
Marion B. H. Whyte, O.B.E., M.A.
W. Stuart Wilkinson
Gillian Williamson
Roger S. Windsor
I. Wotherspoon
John N. Wright
J. A. Younger

AN
ACCOUNT
OF
FIVE AERIAL VOYAGES
IN
SCOTLAND,
IN A
SERIES OF LETTERS
TO HIS
GUARDIAN,
CHEVALIER GERARDO COMPAGNI,

WRITTEN UNDER THE IMPRESSION OF THE VARIOUS EVENTS THAT AFFECTED THE UNDERTAKING,

By VINCENT LUNARDI, Esq.

Secretary to the late Neapolitan Ambaſſador, Firſt Aerial Traveller in England, an Honorary Member of the Hon. Artillery Company of the City of London, Royal Archer of Scotland, Citizen of Edinburgh, Cupar, St. Andrew's, Hawick, &c. &c.

J. BELL, Bookseller to His Royal Highness the PRINCE of WALES.

LONDON:
PRINTED FOR THE AUTHOR, AND SOLD BY J. BELL, BOOKSELLER TO HIS ROYAL HIGHNESS THE PRINCE OF WALES, AND J. CREECH EDINBURGH.

M DCC LXXXVI.

TO THE

DUKE AND DUCHESS

OF

BUCCLEUGH.

My Lord Duke, and my Lady Duchess,

I AM only a Student in the Language of Britain, and wholly unacquainted with that Dialect of it which is appropriated to Dedications.

In my Aerial Voyages in Scotland, I was treated with general Favour. This I attributed in some measure to the Character of the Nation; but principally to the Protection and Countenance of the Duke and Duchess of Buccleugh.

If I were to enumerate your private and public Virtues, I should only whisper feebly what now employs the general Voice of your Country.

I am

I am a Child of Britain only by a Species of Adoption; my Opinion and Praises can have little Weight; and I may be soon dissipated in that Region for which I have a Strong Predilection. Whatever be my Fate, Sentiments of Gratitude to the DUKE and DUCHESS of BUCCLEUGH, will be among the Last Feelings of my Heart.

I have the Honor to be,

My LORD DUKE, and my LADY DUCHESS,

Your GRACES

most obliged

and most devoted Servant,

VINCENT LUNARDI.

LONDON, *May* 2, 1786.

LETTER I.

Edinburgh, Sept. 15. 1785.

MY DEAREST FRIEND,

CARESSED by the ENGLISH NATION, and flattered by the voice of Fame, with pleasures and honours courting my acceptance, does it not afford matter for speculation and surprise, that I should leave a *land*, to which my heart is engaged by numberless endearing ties, for one where only report had made me known? Yes, my honoured, my respected Guardian, I am now in SCOTLAND; and Heaven be praised that I am! It is what I have long wished, and that wish was founded on reason and gratitude.

Amongst the numbers who, in ENGLAND, honoured me with the strongest proofs of sincere regard, were many of the SCOTTISH NATION: these I found, upon all occasions, my *real* friends; most of them were at once men of science and liberality. From an uniformity of virtues in the characters of those individuals I had the happiness to be acquainted with, I judged of, and esteemed the *whole Nation.* Long were my thoughts bent on going to that Country, where my imagination had formed the idea of meeting many whose hearts beat congenial to my own: GLORY too co-operated with my feelings; I should be *the first Aeronaut in* SCOTLAND; it was an inspiring thought! I should at once indulge the emotions of humanity, and eternize my name in that land, where history and poetry have delivered their *forceful lessons* in native strength and purity, through the long, long annals of time.

On the *northern bounds* of ENGLAND are still to be seen the remains of a strong wall, first begun by the *Emperor* ADRIAN, and afterwards continued by SEVERUS, to secure the ROMANS the possession of their conquest, by preventing the incursions of the PICTS and SCOTTS: the *first* they might have looked upon as inconsiderable enemies; but the *latter* were far more formidable. They were a NATION which had never been conquered; a *hardy race,* inured to toil beneath inclement skies:—They knew neither the *arts* nor the *vices* which COMMERCE scatters intermixed with her blessings. The *Chace* was their employment and support. Their chief weapons, for offence, were a kind of darts or javelins; for defence they used a light buckler or shield. Their amusement was to listen to the *songs* of their BARDS, who related the *actions* of HEROES, and their highest glory to leave the fame of some great action behind them, which might be handed down to posterity by those historians. Their *descendents,* with more civilized manners, inherit their virtues; and the *Amor Patriæ* glows in every CALEDONIAN's BOSOM.

I had a most delightful journey from LIVERPOOL hither. It is now the season of the year when the

warm

warm tints of Autumn embellish the face of nature, I viewed with pleasure the surrounding objects. The trees, not yet stripped of their leafy honours, raised their heads in variegated hues; and the verdant garments of the meadows, bordered with embrowning hedges, formed a beautiful contrast to the rich yellow which enrobed the stubble fields. How lovely is nature to an eye unjaundiced by a sickly immagination!

<blockquote>
A wayward fancy courts the pow'rs of art;
But Nature's charms alone can touch the heart.
</blockquote>

As I proceeded *Northward* the fences and inclosures of lime-stone had at first rather a disagreeable effect; but this was amply recompensed by the delightful scenery which now struck my sight! rising hills covered with short grass and aromatic herbage, which afforded pasturage to innumerable flocks of sheep; deep, but smiling vallies, cultivated by the hand of industry, and a distant range of *almost Alpine* mountains rising one behind another, and mingling their blue summits with the clouds. I could almost have imagined myself in the enchanted *regions of romance*; in some of those situations so forcibly described by our countryman ARIOSTO, whose works, through succeeding ages, have gained him the epithet of DIVINE. The ruins of some time mouldered castle, or decayed monastery, now and then checquering the scene, added strength to the powers of fancy. Perhaps from one of these, seated on a towering hill, some *lordly* BARON, in former times, looked down, with proud insolence on the vassals of his power who held all their worldly goods

goods, nay almoſt their *very lives* but as precarious tenures under an imperious maſter. Perhaps in another,—but hold my pen; the theme is not for thee: let us leave it to *ſchoolmen* and *divines*; I am happy in holding this opinion, that RELIGION is not the leſs lovely in herſelf becauſe *different nations* chuſe to repreſent her in *different habits*.

As I approached EDINBURGH the landſcape grew ſtill more picturesque and claimed my higheſt admiration! A croud of mingled ſenſations now ruſhed upon my heart; curioſity, joy, friendſhip, expectation, the love of fame, and diffidence of ſuccefs, created a tumult there; but Hope, ſmiling Hope, Queen of the Paſſions, aſſumed her reign, and huſhed them all to peace!

I entered *this city* on the 12th of this month. It forms nearly an oblong ſquare, with the CASTLE at one end, and the palace of HOLYROOD-HOUSE at the other, and two large wings projecting from the ſides; the NEW-TOWN on the *North*, and SUBURBS on the *South*. It appears to have been begun in early ages, on the moſt foutherly part of that eminence where the caſtle now ſtands; and ſpreading gradually from thence, now covers three ſmall hills or ridges: the OLD TOWN being ſituated on the middle one, the NEW TOWN on that to the North, and the ſuburbs to the South. The difficulty of paſſing betwixt the two former gave riſe to a ſcheme, which was executed ſome years ago, of joining them by a magnificent bridge: a ſimilar one is now carrying on to facilitate a communication with the SUBURBS. Time in his flight over this city has continually ſcattered from his wings

an

an increase of prosperity: may it ever enjoy that blessing; and through all succeeding ages be, as it now is, the residence of true NOBILITY, BENEVOLENCE, and HOSPITALITY.

I have apartments in WALKER's HOTEL, in PRINCE's STREET, NEW TOWN, from whence I behold innumerable elegant buildings, and my ears are saluted with the sounds of industry from many others emulously rising. HAIL to the VOICE of LABOUR! it vibrates more forcibly on the chords of my heart, than the most harmonious notes of music, and gives birth to sensations that I would not exchange for all the boasted pleasures of LUXURY and DISSIPATION. What a sweet sympathy gladdens my breast when I bebehold the *thousands* of *honest workmen* returning, from the toil of the day, with the smiles of content diffused over their countenances; who, but for this employment, might have been exposed to all the miseries of want, and heard their famished babes lament in vain! *Gracious God!* how does thy divine Providence ordain so many different modes of subsistence suited to the various necessities of thy creatures. I cannot express what my soul feels, when even in my Imagination I behold the FATHER of a FAMILY sit down with pleasure to the hard earned meal, surrounded by a numerous offspring; his dwelling is the dwelling of chearfulness, and health, and contentment, preside at his homely board, such are the blessings of industry; you will judge how wide they are scattered here when I inform you that the buildings carried on in this city, employ 1500 workmen, and the expences are estimated not less than 60,000l. sterling *per annum*.

It

It would be an endless task for me to describe the PUBLIC EDIFICES and SEMINARIES of LEARNING for which *Edinburgh* is so justly celebrated, or the *well regulated* POLICE by which it is governed: I know it will afford you more pleasure to learn that I am peculiarly happy, and treated with uncommon *politeness* and *hospitality*; my arrival was no sooner announced than many GENTLEMEN of *distinction* honoured me with their visits; and I am hourly receiving *cards* of *invitation* from the *first families* in EDINBURG; but the most engaging company, and the most flattering compliments, can never make me forget how much I am, and ever must be

Your obliged and grateful,

VINCENT LUNARDI.

LETTER II.

Edinburgh, Sept. 20. 1785.

MY HONOURED FRIEND,

I Do not fear, I do not imagine, that you will think me tedious in giving you a minute account of every circumstance relative to my undertaking. This is not the suggestion of vanity; it arises from the firm dependence I have upon your affection, an

affection

affection founded upon a permanent bafis, and proof againft the united force of time and abfence.

Since my laft, I have been looking out for a place to afcend from, and of confequence, have had many agreeable rambles in and about EDINBURGH, which, with every advantage that art can give, enjoys thofe of nature in a fuperlative degree. Moft *cities* are furnifhed with *public walks*, where the inhabitants may enjoy the frefh air; but here you ftep at once from the noife and buftle of a large *city* into the moft romantic folitude. The CALTON HILL, ARTHUR SEAT, and the adjoining eminences, afford retreats where the graveft philofopher may indulge his contemplations; the melancholy mourner, fequeftered from the prying eye of bufy curiofity, pour fourth his fighs in filence to the paffing winds; or the enraptured poet *catch infpiration*! For my part, I am fo much an inhabitant of the etherial regions, that my ideas already antecipate the pleafure I hope foon to enjoy, in beholding from various *angles* of *elevation*, the *fpires* of EDINBURGH, and the hills of ARTHUR SEAT and CALTON; but above all, the neighbouring FRITH of FORTH, which runs a vaft way into the country. Objects like thefe, united in one view, muft form a fcene, the magnificence of which cannot be conceived by any but an *aërial traveller*. I have now another opportunity before me of gratifying my ambition, by croffing this *branch* of the *fea*, fhould the wind prove favourable; my earneft wifhes are for a breeze from the *fouth* or *fouth-eaft*; the *gentle breath* of ZEPHYRUS I am at prefent ambitious of courting, left it

fhould

should waft me to the GERMAN OCEAN; a journey through which, it is possible my pinions might not be able to carry me.

In my walks round the city, I have observed many places from whence I might conveniently ascend; but my wishes are ultimately turned towards obtaining a large area on the south-west side of the town, named GEORGE'S SQUARE, environed with elegant buildings: there are seven avenues to it from the streets, which might be shut up at a very trifling expence: in the middle is a green plot, encompassed with iron rails, capable of containing several thousand people: and the circumjacent windows offer such convenient accomodations for the Ladies to behold the ascension, that I shall be severely mortified if I cannot be permitted to launch my Balloon from this Square.

I am now happy in the acquaintance of the Hon. HENRY ERSKINE, Sir WILLIAM FORBES, and MAJOR FRAZER, whose politeness and friendship I already experience in an eminent degree: their confidence in my success is boundless! On communicating my desire of ascending from GEORGE's-SQUARE to Mr. ERSKINE, who is himself an inhabitant of it, he kindly promised to exert his utmost interest on my behalf, and I doubt not but he will succeed.

I have been advised, by all my friends, to open a subscription in order to defray all my expences, which must of necessity be very considerable; with this view I have advertised that I will ascend as soon as a competent sum can be raised.

Every

Every thing succeeds according to my most sanguine wishes, and the *sunshine* of *success* gilds my *prospects*. I begin to hope, that I shall go through this enterprize without a single disappointment; what a novelty will that be to me! When I take a retrospective view of my life, I find *misfortune* ushering in every great event; but I think she is now tired of her office, and means to give me some little respite: that she may never cross your path, is the sincere prayer of him who, with the truest affection, bids you adieu, and must ever remain

Your grateful

V. LUNARDI.

———————

LETTER III.

Edinburgh, Sept. 28. 1785.

MY DEAR GUARDIAN,

SHARE my joy; participate my pleasures! SCOTLAND cannot boast a *happier man* than your friend. I can assure you, that I rise some inches taller to take a more extensive view of my delightful prospects! Does not your *mind's eye* behold me, soaring on rapture's bright wings to the summit of happiness, and laughing at the clouds of care below?

You will say, and with reason, (pardon the pun), that I am *flighty* : but how, my *dear, dear Friend,* how can I help it, when my spirits are light as the soft Gossamour that floats on the summer breeze ?

I shall indubitably ascend from the very place I wish. My valuable friend, Mr. ERSKINE, has called a meeting of all the inhabitants of GEORGE's SQUARE, who are now in town, and they are unanimous in my favour: being themselves the proprietors, they can give me permission to go up from thence without infringing any of the city right's: it is impossible for any thing but the weather to disappoint me, and from that I shall be extremely well sheltered.

Upon hearing the news of Mr. ERSKINE's success, I went immediately, accompanined by Mr. SPOTTISWOOD, to measure the seven avenues, and calculate the expence of closing them, leaving two passages large enough for the admission of carriages. Several carpenters to whom I applied declined the task; but at length Mr. MITCHELL succeeded in procuring one who wrote me the following note;

" *Franc Braidwood's best Compliments to Mr. Lu-*
" *nardi, begs leave to inform him that, after calculating*
" *the expence of inclosing the seven openings to Georges's*
" *Square, with strong iron railings from* 10 *to* 12 *feet*
" *high, with gateways to admit carriages, it will amount*
" *to thirty pounds sterling. If very little damage is done*
" *by the crowd, perhaps to a few pounds less..*

" *Luckenbooths, Monday, Sept.* 26. 1785.

With

With this proposal I instantly closed, and ordered the work to be carried on without loss of time, as my intention is to ascend as soon as possible.

My servants are just arrived with the airy Vehicle, which is destined to convey me to the temple of Fame; or, in other words, with my Baloon. The apparatus for filling it will be here on Thursday evening, as the waggoner contracted with my servants to bring it from LIVERPOOL in ten days. George's Square is large enough to contain a sufficient number of spectators to defray my expences at a very trifling price of admission; therefore I shall not wait for the supscriptions being full, but advertise my ascent for the 5th of October next, which I hope will be propitious to my glory. I can procure plenty of the *vitriolic acid* here, so that I have nothing now to dread. My soul is calm as the glassy surface of an unruffled lake, and reflects only pleasing images. Tis a fine still night, and the *thick spangled vault of heaven* glitters with unusual brightness: What a season for enthusiasm, to view the planets wheeling in their radient spheres, and to imagine CELESTIAL BEINGS looking down from every orb, and with fond complacency guarding the peaceful slumbers of good men. To your watchful care, oh ye MINISTERS of the great DEITY, I recommend my ever honoured Friend! If there are such Intelligences, who preside over the occurrences of my life, you are sure of their patronage. With that idea in my mind I bid you GOOD NIGHT; and with every cordial wish, subscribe myself
    Truly your's,
     V. LUNARDI.

LETTER IV.

My Honoured Friend. *Sept.* 29. 1785.

I HAVE now abundant reason to reflect on the *instability* of *human fortune,* which, like the waves of a stormy ocean, only raises us one moment that we may sink into a deeper abyss the next. Could you have imagined from my last, that I should so soon suffer a sad reverse? But such is my fate; and when I wrote that " *I laughed at the clouds of care below me*;" little did I imagine, that they would rise and overshadow my brightest hopes.

With a mind tuned to the highest pitch of joy, in the full flow of exhilarated spirits, I penned an advertisement, which appeared in yesterday's newspaper, assuring the PUBLIC that I would ascend, at all events, on the 5th instant.

But how was my soul depressed, when a friend of mine assured me, that an opposition was forming to deprive me of the pleasure I hoped to receive in ascending from GEORGE's SQUARE, and advised me to stop the carpenter's work immediately, that I might not incur an expence which would certainly be to no purpose. Scarce knowing whether to credit the report or not, with all my thoughts stretched on the rack of suspense, I waited on Mr. ERSKINE. Ever prompt to acts of benevolence, his utmost efforts are exerted to aleviate distress wherever he finds it. Need I tell you that he has taken the trouble to enquire minutely

minutely into this affair? And the result of his enquiries is, O Heaven! it is, that I am to give up all hopes of obtaining this favourable situation to ascend from. What shall I do? I am almost mad, and scarce know what I write; forgive my impetuosity; I cannot just now proceed; I will resume my pen when I am a little more calm.

* * * * * * * * * * * *

Reason tells me that some concealed enemy lurks at the bottom of this mischief: But who can that enemy be? So may I prosper as I declare, in all sincerity, I do not know the creature I have intentionally wronged. And can it be in the power of human nature to be guilty of such malevolent actions, without the smallest provocation? I am detetermined, at all events, to find out this *incendiary* who has taken such pains to impede my happiness: for, in every disappointment, it is natural to indulge a curiosity concerning the cause, however little the knowledge of it may conduce to a remedy.

* * * * * * * * * * * *

Worse and worse my dear Friend! Could you have conceived it possible, that the underhand prompter of my disappointment was a LADY? My sole motive in applying for GEORGE's SQUARE, was the better accommodation of the LADIES; and, though they might not have honoured this little attention with their particular notice, yet I could never have imagined that a positive opposition to my darling scheme would have originated with them: With *them* did I say?

say? Hold; I beg pardon of the FAIR SEX; *they are* my *best friends*, and I prize *their approbation* beyond the highest honours fame can give! and shall a FE-MALE MACHIAVEL of *fifty* be ranked with *them*? Forbid it *politeness*; forbid it *humanity*; forbid it TRUTH! I am happy in reflecting, that the *young*, the *fair*, and the *amiable* have never been my enemies; and that my opponent is

> Not she whose lips the fragrant rose adorns,
> Whose tender heart each angry passion scorns,
> In whose bright eyes Love's subtle light'nings play,
> Whose smiles enchant with graces ever gay;
> But she on whom the *wild December* pours
> The chilling influence of his icy show'rs,
> Whose *fifty winters* have effac'd her charms,
> And frowning sent her from their shrivell'd arms.

However severe my disappointment, it is in some degree alleviated by the *picture* I have here drawn of its AUTHORESS; which, I assure you, is not in the least bordering upon *caricature*: and as I do not imagine myself able either to subdue, or stand before the SPIRIT of CONTRADICTION, I have determined, reluctantly determined, to relinquish all hopes of obtaining what I so ardently wished.

I must now endeavour to procure some other place to ascend from, nor will I close this letter till I can inform you of my success.

* * * * * * * * * * * * * *

The dawn of hope again disperses the clouds of vexation; I have procured a convenient situation for
launching

launching my Balloon: but this is anticipating events, and I have promised to give you a regular account of all my proceedings.

After relinquishing all thoughts of GEORGE's-SQUARE, my wishes turned towards the COLLEGE, where is an area which I imagined might answer very well: thither my kind friend Mr. ERSKINE, accompanied me, and, after measuring it and fixing on the most eligible spot, he waited on several of the PROFESSORS, who politely gave their consent, but had it not in their power to guarantee the completion of my wishes, as that must ultimately depend upon the LORD PROVOST. Sir WM. FORBES had done me the honour of introducing me to his *Lordship*, from whom I had received civilties beyond my most sanguine expectations, I therefore flew with pleasure to inform him of my desire, and obtain his assent; but found, to my no small surprize, that he was already acquainted with the whole transaction: *A certain Artist* belonging to the COLLEGE, having got intelligence of my application for that place, had been beforehand with me; and, pretending that the roofs of several adjacent houses might be damaged by the mob, effectually prevented my being successful on this occasion. His *Lordship* represented the whole affair in a proper light, and with a candour, which reflected the highest honour on his humanity, appealed to myself whether it was in his power to grant my request.

From the depression of spirits, attending this second disappointment, I was rouzed by the kindness of Sir WM. FORBES who intimated, that, being one of the

mana-

managers of the Infirmary, he might possibly have it in his power to procure me the garden belonging to that building: It is a magnificent structure admirably well adapted to the purposes for which it rose. The garden I saw and approved; my *worthy friend* wrote to the other *managers* for their joint consent: and I had every reason in the world to hope for a favourable answer.

According to appointment I called this morning at the *Writing-Office*; but, to my severe mortification, the answer was still in the *negative*. The Lord Provost however informed me that I might perhaps obtain the gardens of Herriot's Hospital, and as he was going out of town, requested Sir W. Forbes to write a letter for me to the managers, who having heard my story, and read the advertisement, immediately complied with my request. Thus, with a little friendly assistance I have surmounted those difficulties which almost warped my brain! Every thing now will go on well; I must advertise immediately, and as I fear being too late for the post, I hasten to subscribe myself

Your ever affectionate,
V. LUNARDI.

Friday Morning, Two o'Clock.

I AM now the most *disconsolate*, the most *wretched being* in the world! the place is fixed, the advertisements are gone out, and all Scotland waits, with anxious expectation, to see me go up on Wednesday next

next: but how, my dearest friend, how shall I keep my *engagements* with the PUBLIC! I am sorry this letter was too late for the post last night! had it gone you would not have suffered so much uneasiness on my account; but now I cannot help communicating to you, the *friend* of my *heart*, my distressed situation! How shall I fill the Balloon ? the apparatus, which should have been here Yesterday, will not arrive till the evening of the day I have appointed to ascend. I sent my servant, last night, to the place where the waggon puts up, and the innkeeper told him that I was mistaken; that it required 16 Days to come from LIVERPOOL hither, and if the WAGGONER said otherwise, it was only in order to secure to himself some emolument from the carriage. I wish you were near me! What shall I do? What apology offer for *deferring* my VOYAGE? I can resolve upon nothing: I fear no very large casks can be procured here, and the time is too short to make new ones. Numbers of people will come from GLASGOW and ABERDEEN and they must all be disappointed! *Maledictus Homo quis confidit in Homo!* Oh what a frame of mind am I in! Every gentler emotion has quitted my breast and all is perturbation there.—The live-long night sleep has refused to visit my pillow, I have risen from it with loathing.— The sickly light of a glimmering taper lends its assistance while I thus pour out my *anguish* in the *bosom* of friendship.

Just now I walked to the window; the *fires* of *Heaven* shine faintly through the thin vapours :—Darkness has not yet withdrawn her veil from the face of the earth;

D

earth; an univerfal *ftillnefs* reigns over this GREAT CI-
TY. Not even the hoarfe barking of the watch-dog,
or the irregular fteps of inebriety, break through the
gloomy filence! my ear cannot catch a fingle found
fave that of the *rufhing wind:* at this ftill hour

> "The bufy founds of population fail,
> "No chearful murmurs fluctuate on the gale."

Nature feems funk in repofe; even the *wicked* are enjoying the fweets of flumber; whilft I alone am waking
a prey to *vexation* and *anxiety!* FAME and GLORY, ye
objects of my *purfuits,* ye deftroy my *peace* of *mind,*
yet are ye ftill *dear* to me! And muft I now lofe the
credit I thought fo well eftablifhed? DESPERATION
is in the idea and I will not encourage it! I will fly to
my *fupreme Protector,* I will humble my foul in the
duft before him: the GREAT GOD of the UNIVERSE
will not refufe to hear the *meaneft* of his *creatures;*
then why fhould I defpond?

* * * * * * * * * * * * * *

I am more calm my friend; but I cannot yet form
any refolution how to act. The grey light of morning dapples the Eaft, and the fmoke begins to rife
in thick volumes, from the chimneys of this *populous*
CITY. I will take a walk; CHANCE may perhaps do
more for me *than* REFLECTION.

Eleven o'Clock Forenoon

Upon laying down my pen this morning, I rambled
through the *ftreets* of the OLD and NEW Towns:
but

but all was still; not a *creature* was stirring. I firmly believe that could I have met ONE HUMAN BEING, though the *veriest wretch* in NATURE; I should have sought relief by complaining to him as to a *bosom friend!* but I was compelled to wander in solitary silence; and with the *cloud* of *vexation* still hanging on my brow, I turned, with reluctant steps, towards my HOTEL.——
Sweet SENSIBILITY! *Queen* of the VIRTUES! thy *dwelling* is not always in the breasts of the RICH, the GREAT, or the LEARNED: often dost thou animate the heart of the *simple* VILLAGER, the *laborious* PEASANT, or the *humble* SLAVE! this I experienced on returning to my lodgings: A *poor girl,* imployed in the *most menial* offices, whose ideas perhaps had never soared above her present station, in the *heart-touching tone* of *unaffected* SYMPATHY, endeavoured to soothe the agitation too visible in my countenance! NATURE is ever the *same,* and the VOICE of HUMANITY is always *dear* to her! I felt its force, and yielded my soul to the pleasing influence! I recapitulated my distresses to the poor but honest creature! and, by her advice, applyed to some dyers whose business required very large Vats: they shewed me some tubs, which were indeed of a proper size, but unluckily had been constructed in the very place where they stood, and consequently must either be taken to pieces or a hole made in the wall to remove them: thus I was left in my former dilemma, nor have I yet hit on any expedient to free me from it.

Evening,

Evening, Eight o'Clock.

I shall at least conclude my letter with some agreeable intelligence: About twelve o'clock I had the good fortune to meet with one Mr. CHALMERS, a plumber, to whom I represented the necessity I was under of keeping my engagements with the public, and entreated him to make me two cisterns, fourteen feet long, four deep, and as many wide: he required a few hours for consideration, and at four o'clock in the afternoon, returned with the joyful news that he would undertake to compleat the task within the limited time, and laid before me an exact *estimate* of the *expence*; I immediately drew up the following bond, with a pencil, and Mr. CHALMERS signed it.

"*I promise to make two cisterns fourteen feet long, four deep, and four wide each, of lead of eight pounds weight a square foot, soldering and air tide, &c. these to be compleated for Tuesday morning before noon of the fourth instant, and the whole for* 20*l. sterling, the lead to be returned as my property.*

W. CHALMERS, PLUMBER."

And now, my *dear guardian*, you will naturally conclude that I look upon Mr. CHALMERS as one of my best friends; indeed he has raised my *spirits* from the *lowest depth* of *despondency*.

I must not omit to give you the pleasing information that LORD ELPHINSTONE has honoured me with a particular mark of his *attention* and *regard*, by ordering the flag to be hoisted, and guns to be fired from the CASTLE on the day of my ascension; and, as he cannot be in town at that time, he has requested COLONEL COCK-

Cockran to grant me a sufficient number of the military, for a guard, as well as to favour me in other respects. The Colonel is a most agreeable veteran officer! and I experienced a peculiar pleasure in speaking Italian with him.

Though I have suffered so many *disappointments*, I cannot ultimately consider myself as unforunate. Adversity, when past, gives a relish to pleasure; and I feel myself more happy, at this moment, than if an uninterrupted success had attended all my schemes. The storm is blown over, and a sweet calm reigns in my heart, tremblingly alive to every soft sensation. You will shew my dear sisters this letter; they will sympathize in my distresses, and they will share in my happiness. I cannot give you a better idea of my present state of mind than in the following lines, which are part of a poem translated by a *friend* of mine, from the works of the celebrated Ossian:

" Like the clear moon in silent night;
" Calm as the lake's unruffled breast,
" When, on the liquid expanse bright,
" The stormy winds are hush'd to rest.

Good night; may peaceful slumbers seal your eye lids, and may you ever enjoy delights like those which now smile on

Your

VINCENT LUNARDI.

LETTER V.

Edinburgh, October, 3. 1785.

MY HONOURED FRIEND,

HOW chequered is the scene of life in which I act! and what vicissitudes of joy and woe do I experience! FORTUNE makes me her sport: one minute she raises me aloft on the airy pinions of hope, the next precipitates me into the fathomless abyss of despair.

Mr. CHALMERS had promised to attend me this morning, in HERRIOT'S GARDEN, at seven o'clock: such confidence had I in his integrity, that I went thither at *one*, with the workmen to make the ditch, and waited the appointed hour: Seven o'clock came; eight, nine, and ten followed; but no news of Mr. Chalmers: At length, when my patience was quite exhausted, he came about eleven, and informed me that he could not execute the task he had undertaken, because his men were employed in making pipes for the NEW STREET. Such an answer from one who had, after mature deliberation, signed his name to a bond, was astonishing! nor could I believe that he was serious, till he had repeated the same words several times, with the most provoking indifference! Upon this my patience forsook me, and I loaded him with the bitterest invectives that rage and disappointment could prompt; but they were all thrown away upon this phlegmatic mortal; he quietly maintained

his

his *sang froid*, and I found it impossible to provoke him even to the smallest degree of discomposure.

Do you think those *beings* happier who possess so much APATHY? Their passage through life is certainly smoother: It is like travelling over an extensive plain, covered with perpetual verdure, and bounded by the horrizon; no various objects strike the view, but all is *universal sweetness:* The MAN of STRONG PASSIONS, though he may be wounded by the asperities of a rugged road, torn by intercepting brambles, or now and then in danger of falling down a precipice, enjoys nobler prospects, and rises to more elevated situations! Even now, surrounded as I am with *distresses* and *perplexities,* and tottering on the brink of a *total disappointment,* I would not relinquish sensibility for the empire of the world! Without SENSIBILITY, *fame, riches, glory,* were *empty sounds!* Joys talked of, but never felt: It is that which animates me, and bids me still look for hope, though I know not which way to turn my face to find her: Adieu! for the present; when I have met with her I will resume my pen.

Tuesday, October 4.

WHEN I quitted my writing, I had the good fortune to meet Mr. ERSKINE, who directed me to Mr. SALBY, another plumber, who, being a man of property, might probably have it in his power to make

me

(24)

me an apparatus within the limited time. I found him busied in sending of a quantity of cast lead for the country; but, on hearing my situation, he immediately ordered it to HERRIOT's GARDEN, where I left him engaged in making draughts for the cisterns, &c. but not till he had given me the most solemn assurances, that every thing should be ready for my ascension at the appointed time.

From thence I went, with a light heart, to the PARLIAMENT HOUSE, where my Balloon is exhibited, being in a happy frame of mind for enjoying the conversation of the LADIES, no less than two hundred of whom have honoured me with their company this morning. Happy mortal! you exclaim:—and well you might, could you form any adequate idea of the SCOTTIH BEAUTIES! Their *heighth* in general approaches to what I should call the MAJESTIC, adorned with an easy elegance; their FIGURES are such as *Grecian Artists* might have been proud to copy! *symmirety* and *proportion* are there displayed in their utmost perfection. But to describe their FACES!— The pencil of TITIAN, or MICHAEL ANGELO, could scarce have done them justice! The GOD of LOVE hides himself in the dimples that play about their mouths: No *perfume shop* supplies the *beautiful colour* that glows on their cheeks and lips; it is the *pure painting* of *health*; and pictures forth *minds as pure.* NATURE has made them lovely, and they have not suffered the *intruder* ART to spoil her works.

I have endeavoured to give you some faint idea of their *personal charms*; but their *mental ones* are far

more

more striking! *Grace* without *affectation*, *frankness* without *levity*, *good-humour* without *folly*, and *dignity* without *pride*, are their distinguishing characteristics. Do you not think this is a fiery ardeal for my heart?—I assure you no: they are all so *very amiable*, that I cannot attach myself to *any* ONE in *particular*: I love them all; and shall court their general approbation with as much ardour as the most empassioned lover would that of his mistress. Ah! what glory to ascend my AERIAL CHARIOT in their view! to be the object of *their* admiration! to have all their eyes turned towards me! all their prayers and wishes breathed forth for my safety! and to hear their united acclamations! Oh Heaven! my very brain turns giddy with the thought, and my whole soul anticipates the happy moment!

I have just received letters from *three* LADIES, expressing their wishes to accompany me in my voyage; but I must of necessity refuse myself that gratification. How unfortonate that the Balloon should be too small to ascend with more than one person! and I have not time to enlarge it, or else,———I am interrupted:—Good God! a message from HERRIOT's GARDEN, requiring my immediate attendance! What can be the matter? How I tremble! Perhaps some unforseen accident,—but I will not torment myself with conjectures;—Adieu.

* * * * * * * * * * *

I am just returned: Mr. Salby only sent for me to view one of the cisterns, which is now finished;

and he assures me that the whole shall be compleated before he leaves the spot. The oil of vitriol, iron, blocks, ropes, &c. &c. are in the Garden; and, for this night, I may repose in security. If I have opportunity, before I ascend, I will write a few lines to let you know what prospects of success attend.

Your

V. LUNARDI.

Tuesday Evening, 8 *o'clock.*

P. S. Surely the world is not to be trusted in any one instance! I had scarce dispatched my letter to the Post Office, when I received the following card; upon which I sent for it back again, that I might acquaint you with the contents.

C A R D.

" COLONEL COCKRANE presents compliments to
" Mr. LUNARDI; it would mortify him greately,
" that either he or the public should meet with a
" disappointment: he waits, with impatience, to
" know the *Commander in Chief's* pleasure, as he finds
" Lord Elphingstone is not expected soon, and the
" COLONEL can neither order guns to be fired, or
" the flag to be hoisted, but by orders from GENE-
" RAL MACKAY.
" *Edinburgh Castle, October* 4.

" A contrary wind would give time to have an
" answer."

It

It gives me pain to conclude with this difagreeable information. It is a difficulty I know not how to furmount; but I muft endeavour to find out fome way: Once more good night.

LETTER VI.

Edinburgh, Wednefday, October 5. 1785.

DEAR FRIEND,

I Difpatched my laft in great anxiety; and, after racking my thoughts to no purpofe, threw myfelf, overcome with fatigue, upon a fopha: configning every care to forgetfulnefs: I enjoyed a calm fleep about twenty minutes: I then rofe, and waited on MAJOR FRAZER, to whom I related my cafe, and told him I apprehended it would be an unpardonable breach of my promife if the flag were not hoifted and the guns fired; as I fhould never have advertifed to that purport, if LORD ELPHINSTONE had not affured me they might be obtained. I had formed a very high idea of the MAJOR's character from the firft moment I had the pleafure of being introduced to him; his politenefs and humanity, on this occafion fully juftified my opinion: He immediately fent a meffage to the NEW BATTERY at LEITH, for a piece of ordnance to be carried up before HERRIOT's HOSPITAL; and kindly inviting me to fup with him, defired that every thing elfe might be left to his care.

Thus relieved from my anxiety, I spent the night in peaceful repose, and awoke with the most beautiful dawn I ever beheld!

> Hail to the rising Sun! whose chearful orb
> Spreads wide the day; whose cloud-dispelling beams
> Shall paint *my prospects*, and illume *my fame*!

All hail to the joyous Light! I feel it in my soul! and praise the *beneficent* CREATOR, whose over-ruling power so wisely divided it from darkness! safe in *his* merciful protection, I will now haste to prepare for the happy moment, when soaring through trackless ether, I shall take a more *extensive survey* of his WONDEROUS WORKS.

Herriot's Garden, 9 o'clock.

I have just received a card from the MAJOR, informing me that, as his interposition in my behalf has proved successful, I may send an order to have the flag hoisted when I think proper.

I have not yet positively resolved to ascend; for, though the weather is very favourable, the wind is contrary, and threatens to drive me into the German Ocean: But people of the first distinction are every minute sending to enquire my determination, Mr. CORRI, an Italian friend, has received a message, from the DUKE and DUCHESS of BUCCLEUGH, to know whether I mean to make the experiment or not.

The

The cafe under its present circumstances, requires some deliberation. At this moment what would I not give to purchase your company; to be assisted by your advice!—One way or other I must resolve.

Half past Eleven.

There are numbers of very respectable people already in the Garden. I have sent Mr. CORRI to acquaint their GRACES, that I hope to be honoured with their presence soon after one o'clock; and begged that he would order some boats to be sent out from Leith, in case of any accident, as the wind is still S. W.

I have requested the attendance of the military, and ordered the gun to be fired and the flag hoisted. The fear of disappointing the *public curiosity*, which is now highly raised, has outweighed every other consideration; and, though the LORD PROVOST gave me a fresh proof of the most flattering regard, by intimating, that he would procure me the indulgence of the public by postponing the day; yet, with the utmost gratitude for his kindness, I declined the offer, and determined at all events to ascend; hoping that some of the boats would take me up, in case my descent should be upon the ocean.

Adieu! my dear friend! I must now prepare to fill the BALLOON. Do not let my sisters know any thing of this letter till you hear from me again. Credit not

too

too haſtily any information you may receive from ſtrangers; though I have the ſtrongeſt hopes the firſt that reaches you will be from

VINCENT LUNARDI.

LETTER VII.

Cupar in Fife, Wedneſday evening, October 5.

MY EVER HONOURED FRIEND,

MY pleaſure will not be complete till I have performed the duties of gratitude, by writing a few lines both to you and to my well wiſhers in EDINBURGH; all of whom, and in particular the LORD PROVOST, Sir WILLIAM FORBES, and MAJOR FRAZER, will be anxious for my ſafety, as they muſt have obſerved my courſe to be directly over the Frith of Forth.

I alighted gently, in a field at a place called CERES, near this town, after a moſt delightful and glorious voyage of 46 *miles,* 36 over the *water* and 10 over *land,* and was received with the moſt affecting demonſtrations of joy.

Excuſe me from writing any more; my next ſhall contain a full account of my excurſion: at preſent this will ſuffice to remove the anxiety occaſioned by my laſt. I beg you will impart the good news to my

ſiſters,

sisters, and assure them that *fame*, *glory*, and *happiness* all conspire to bless

Your, and their, affectionate

V. LUNARDI.

LETTER VIII.

Melville House, October 7. 1785.

MY DEAR FRIEND,

I NOW proceed to give you the particulars of my late glorious voyage, which in many respects, has been the most remarkable I ever made.

At twelve o'clock, on Wedenesday the 5th of this month, I began the operation of filling the BALOON, with one pipe from each of the cisterns, communicating with another to which the BALLOON was connected: At two o'clock it was sufficiently inflated to carry me, with the ballast, instruments, &c. but the wind still continuing to blow from the S. W. I fastened eight bladders to my car: then, having taken in 60 lb. of ballast, several ropes, a basket of provisions, sent me by Mrs. CORRI, and a cork jacket with which I was furnished by Dr. RAE: I put on my regimentals, and ordered the machine to be carried quite to the *eastern part of the area*, that the LADIES might have a better view of the *ascension*.

Before

Before my departure, I shook hands with Sir WILLIAM FORBES, and requested him to advertise, that I would make another experiment on the Wednesday following, for the benefit of the CHARITY WORK-HOUSE.

At *forty five minutes past three* I left the earth, with a considerable rising power, in order to clear the buildings; but when I had arrived at the heighth of 1100 Feet, and saluted the people below, I thought proper to check this power, by pulling the valve and letting out some of the *inflammable air*.

At this period I excited some anxiety in the minds of the spectators by lowering my flag, which is 40 feet square, and fastened to a string 300 feet long; this they interpreted as a signal of distress. The barometer now stood at 28, and had fallen an inch since my departure. At this elevation I spent some time in contemplating the *beauties* of the *scene* below, which were indeed beyond description! especially to those who have never been in a similar situation! The HILLS about EDINBURGH appeared like *small mounts* raised by *art*, and the *extensive labours* of the neighbouring farmers as so many *gardens*, divided into little *plots*. The CITY of GLASGOW I could plainly distinguish, and also the TOWN of PAISLEY; as well as all those on both *sides* of the Forth, the *meanders* of which, with the HIGHWAYS and RIVERS in the adjacent country, had exactly the same appearance as if laid down on a map; indeed every object seemed to lessen and recede from the eye much more than it would have done if viewed at an equal distance horizontally.

My attention was taken from thefe enchanting profpects by obferving myfelf to be perpendicular over the Frith of Forth: I had been fo immerfed in contemplation that the Balloon had afcended 2000 *feet* without my perceiving it; and, had not the *barometer* been fufpended as high as my head, I might infenfibly have foared totally out of fight.

I had not expended any of the ballaft, and ftill poffeffed fome power of afcenfion, when I faw two boats together, and another about a gun fhot diftance, rowing very faft, and, by the dafhing of their oars, making the water look like filver all around them : I now recollected the order I had given to Mr. Corri; but perceiving they had not gone out to Largo, according to that order, and that there was a ship near the island of May, and another at no very great diftance, I thought proper to defcend, purpofely to difcharge the boats, and gratify my curiofity about the island of Inchkeith. The Balloon turned on its axis all the time I defcended, and having lowered it to within 500 feet of the water, I bid them *good bye*, and told them that it was in vain attempting to keep up with me: then, throwing out a bag of fand, I immediately afcended; and, after taking fome refrefhment, flung down a bottle: all this time I obferved that the Balloon was rifing gently with a direction due eaft. I then opened my bafket of provifions, but do not mean to tell you *how* I *thanked* the lady to whofe politenefs I was fo much indebted, fuffice it to fay, that I made a light but not inelegant repaft; and then entered a thin cloud, about half a mile in length,

length, after my paſſage through which I threw out about three pounds of ballaſt, as the BALLOON had loſt its riſing power, and kept turning gently on its AXIS. Some ſnow had ſettled on it; but, upon being re-expoſed to the ſun beams, this ſoon diſſolved and dropt into the GALLERY. Being now above the cloud I perceived that *it* moved ſlower than the BALLOON, which, to my view, ſeemed perpendicularly over two black ſpots; but I could not determine whether they were diſmaſted ſhips, or rocks near NORTH BERWICK.

I imagined that the wind would carry me over land again; but, upon fixing the quadrant, found that I was yet at leaſt two miles on the water. The flag did not now remain perpendicular, but inclined to the *eaſt*, about 20 yards beyond the BALLOON, the direction of which leant a little to the *weſt*, and the COMPASS with it: Thus I perceived that there were *two contrary* CURRENTS of AIR: and, as it was very dangerous to remain in that with which I ſet out, I reſolved to try whether it was not practicable to return by the upper one, or at leaſt be carried by it over land: However, to prepare for the worſt, I took off my UNIFORM and put on the CORK JACKET, and then threw out a whole bag of ſand, on which the Balloon inſtantly aſcended to an aſtoniſhing height. At forty minutes after three the *barometer* ſtood at 18. 5. the thermometer at 34. and the detached one at 32; the BALLOON and FLAG in one direction, and, by the COMPASS, the wind at *eaſt*.

When thus elevated I could plainly diſtinguiſh all the NORTHERN COAST of BRITAIN; but the clouds

and

and mifts, towards the *south* and *east*, prevented my having any diftinct profpects in either of thofe quarters; fo that the proud-fwelling GERMAN OCEAN was wholly hid from my view; nor could I tell, by the direction of the wind, whether I was receding from, or advancing towards it.

At four o'clock the BALLOON began to defcend gently and, for two minutes, I was enveloped in a cloud fo that I could not behold either the *skies, earth,* or *sea*: In three minutes I could plainly perceive myfelf to be two miles from fhore; and, in another minute, the *barometer* had rifen, from its loweft ftation, to 20 inches, on which I threw away another fmall bottle, and fwept the remainder of the fand off the FLOOR of the GALLERY: by this means I was enabled to proceed in an horizontal direction.

I now faw the ISLAND of INCH-KEITH on my left; the BALLOON and FLAG ftill continuing in one direction and moving towards LARGO: I was overjoyed to find myfelf fo near the completion of my wifhes: the moft ardent hope could not have painted a more fuccefsfu journey, to the fanguine eye of bufy expectation.

At six minutes paft four, perceiving by my quadrant that I was about half a mile over land, I took off my cork jacket with pleafure, put on my uniform, and finding my ftomach in fome degree affected with the cold, drank a glafs of cordial, which I muft own at this moment was not at all unfeafonable. Defcending very gently I had full leifure to contemplate the beautiful profpect: I had not only a charming view of the FRITHS of FORTH and TAY, with the towns on

each

each fide of them but could plainly fee ARBROATH and MONTROSE on the NORTHERN COAST; however the diftant perfpective gradually vanifhed as I approached the earth, and, at 20 *minutes paft four o'clock,* I alighted on the ground as mentioned in my laft.

I was inftantly furrounded by feveral farmers, to whom I had fpoken for fome time through the trumpet: the firft in the habit of a gentleman that reached me was Mr. Robert Chriftie, who politely enquired after my fafety and affifted me in getting out of the gallery; the next was Mr. Mathew, the keeper of the beft inn at Cupar; he feemed to be acquainted with me a great while before, and he did a very great fervice to me; the other was the Reverend Mr. *Arnot,* who, with forty or fifty people, came running quite out of breath. Hah! I am fummoned to affift at a *little* Sacrifice to the PENATES; or, to fpeak in plainer terms, the bell rings for breakfaft: You know my cuftom of rifing early, it has afforded me an opportunity of fcribbling this enormous letter to you, but now I muft for a little while lay down my pen.

I am returned from the *happy* BOARD of *true* HOSPITALITY, where ELEGANCE prefides without SUPERFLUITY, and where the ENJOYMENTS of LIFE continually fmile without betraying to VOLUPTUOUSNESS. Pardon this little digreffion from my narrative; I will now proceed.—With the affiftance of the people who came crouding about me, I foon emptied the BALLOON, which, with its CAR, NETTING, &c. was conveyed, in triumph, to CUPAR TOWN-HALL. I was fupplied
with

with a horfe by Mr. MATHEW of CUPAR, and took my firft refrefhment at Mr. ARNOT's, from whence, accompanied by the two gentlemen above mentioned, feveral others, and four Ladies who came in a carriage to meet me, with the *multitude* of *followers* every moment encreafing, I proceeded to CUPAR, where I was received with JOY truly *inexpreffible* ! The *lower ranks* of *people* looked upon me as a kind of Superior BEING : and Hope, in her fweeteft ftrain of delicate flattery, whifpers in my ear that LUNARDI's ARRIVAL in that country, will be celebrated for many years to come ! At night I was fplendidly entertained with an elegant fupper by the gentlemen of the town.

Yefterday morning I went to fee my BALLOON, and found it torn in feveral places about the neck. I am ftrongly tempted here to mention a circumftance which, however trifling it may feem to you, afforded me infinite pleafure ! I know you will think me vain; but confider my deareft friend, I am a young man ; I have for fome time experienced the praifes, the careffes, nay, even the adulation, of all ranks of people ! Mounted upon the higheft pinacle of Fame's temple, with the loud fhouts of applaufe ringing in my ears; can it excite wonder if my head fhould turn a little giddy ? The joys which univerfal admiration prefents are intoxicating ; but I cannot voluntarily relinquifh them.—Shall I relate this pleafing incident ? I am irrefolute :—Yes : I will : If either that, or any other paffage in my Letters appears too much inclined to *egotifm*, you will behold it through the medium of friendfhip, and pardon the errors of a heart which,

which, with a franknefs too unguarded, yields itfelf to the fenfations of the moment.

I found the Town Hall full of Ladies, who upon my expreffing a defire to have the Balloon mended, vied with each other in lending their affiftance to repair it; fo that, in lefs than half an hour, it was as complete as ever. Delighted with this mark of attention, I told them, in the gaiety of my heart, that they deferved a reward for their labour; and, cutting a number of fmall fhreds from the Neck of the Balloon, prefented one to each of them: but what was my fatisfaction when I beheld thefe trifling *mementos* received with the moft *animated* Expressions of Regard, and placed as little treafures in the Pocket Books of thefe Fair Ones, fome of whom honoured me fo far, as to promife that they would have them fet for rings or lockets, to wear in remembrance of the event which introduced me to their acquaintance.

After this agreeable incident, I was invited to dine with the Provost and Magistrates who prefented me with the Freedom of the Town. The Hospitality of *thefe people* is almoft incredible! as one inftance of it, I muft inclofe you the tranfcript of a lettter fent me by Mr. Grace, *Secretary* to the *Society* of Gentlemen Golfers. I was next honoured with a vifit from Lord Balgonie, who, in the name of his *Father*, *Mother*, and the *whole family*, invited me to their houfe, where I have experienced the utmoft hofpitality and politenefs! The *people* of *diftinction* in Scotland, are bleft with elegance and happinefs, and know not that infatiable ambition
which,

which, while it fwallows up every other comfort and endearment of life, never fails to prove the bane of human blifs: Their enjoyments are chiefly thofe of the domeftic kind; a *virtuous* and *lovely* Wife, the education and company of their Children, and focial joys, participated with their friends, conftitute their principal pleafures.

The chaife is ready; I muft quit this happy *manfion*, and fet out for St. Andrew's. On my arrival at Edinburgh I fhall write you again: till then adieu! and may the God of Goodnefs crown all your undertakings with fuccefs, equal to that which now fmiles upon

Your fincerely affectionate
VINCENT LUNARDI.

To Mr. LUNARDI.

SIR,

" I am defired by the Gentlemen Golfers juft now
" affembled here, to congratulate you upon your fafe
" arrival on this fide of the Forth. The whole of the
" Gentlemen here convened, and in particular thofe
" whofe refidence is in the neighbourhood of Cupar,
" are extremely forry, that by reafon of their abfence,
" they have it not in their power to pay you that at-
" tention

" tention and respect which you are intitled to by
" your merit: They beg leave to follicit your pre-
" fence at St. ANDREW's, which they will confider
" as a particular honour done them.

"I have the honour to be, for the Gentlemen
" Golfers,

" Sir,

" Your most obedient and
" very humble Servant,

" STUART GRACE,

" *Secretary to the Club.*

" *St. Andrews, 6th October* 1785."

LETTER VIII.

Edinburgh, Oct. 15, 1785.

MY EVER HONOURED FRIEND,

I HOPE your own heart will plead my excuse, and suggest that some unavoidable necessity has obliged me to delay writing: when I reflect how many days have elapsed since I dispatched my last Letter, I am astonished at their appearing to fill so small an interval of time! The hours have passed by no swifter than usual, yet, to me their flight has been almost
imperceptible;

imperceptible; fo fully has either bufinefs or pleafure occupied every moment.

A little after noon I reached St. ANDREWS, where I dined with the Gentlemen GOLFERS, and after converfing fome time about my late fuccefsful voyage, I had the honour to be elected a MEMBER of the CLUB, and had the FREEDOM of the TOWN prefented to me by the PROVOST and MAGISTRATES: all thefe ceremonies over, I was conducted to the *Ball Room*, where I found upwards of 100 *beautiful* LADIES already affembled.

I had forgot to mention a fingular accident which happened to me, on my entrance into CUPAR, fimilar to that which formerly befel POPE GANGANELLI on his taking poffeffion of the three kingdoms; a gentleman, in the excefs of his joy, firing a gun too near my horfe, the animal was fo much frightened, that he threw me, and fell with confiderable force upon my knee: I did not, at that moment, feel much inconvenience, but in the night-time I fuffered extremely, and the next day could fcarcely walk: but the fight of fo many beautiful Ladies exhilerated my fpirits to fuch a degree, that, though not yet quite recovered, I totally forgot my recent misfortune, and could not refrain from dancing a minuet with one of the lovely daughters of your *old acquaintance*. I do not recollect ever to have fpent a more agreeable evening.

Next morning I vifited the Univerfity, which is a noble inftitution, furnifhed with a good library, and fome very valuable ancient manufcripts. The remains of the Cathedral Church, though sinking under the repeated strokes of time, exhibit a striking specimen of the heavy Gothic Architecture, which, though far from possessing that symmetry and elegance characteristic of the five regular Orders, yet distinguishes the awful and sublime more strongly than any other kind of building. There is a solemnity steals over the soul upon entering these majectic ruins: What a scene for contempelation! Memory loves the idea, and Fancy pants to pursue it uncontrouled; for once my dear friend indulge me while I give her free scope.

I will carry you with me on the wings of immagination, to this *venerable Pile*, at the solemn hour of midnight, when univerfal nature sleeps. Here we will alight at this nigh tottering wall, whose cleft side *gapes*, a *passage* to admit the traveller. What a meditative silence! it deepens the gloom! How the Moon-light Streams through the tall Arch, where the variegated pane once faintly admitted the lustre of Day! The shadow falls on neglected *tombs* and forgotten *graves*. Let us sit down on this stone; tis the base of a Column long since levelled with the dust: how proudly it stood amongst its compeers supporting the ponderous roof! how excellently that fretted roof re-echoed the Coral Hymns of Praise! Where are their Glories now? Borne away on the broad wings of time, and scattered in the air. Soft! what noise is that? Twas the bat, shrieking as she fluttered by: We have disturbed the obscene tenants of this once hallowed Mansion! The owl sits hooting on the wall. How the hollow ground sounds with
our

our footsteps! We pass over the dreary habitations of the Dead, the dark vaults where the greatest Heroes, Statesmen, and Princes, moulder undistinquished: Ye Conquerors and Lawgivers, the wide *grasp* of your *ambition* is now bounded by the narrow grave! unnoticed and forgotten, ye mingle with yonr native dust, a prey to the meanest of the reptile tribe. while o'er your now unhonoured bones, baleful ARACHNE spreads her subtle web, and cloaths the damp walls of your Prison-house! Peace! how the wind sighs through the blast-worn chinks, and murmurs in the lonely ailes! it tells a mournful tale to Reason's ear, and whispers forth the Mutability of Worldly bliss.

Let us quit this scene, whether we have been transported by the power of fancy, and return to the description of others not less interestesting.

To the west of the Cathedral stands a decayed Castle, built in early ages, and formerly the residence of CARDINAL BEATON, with whose story you are well acquainted: Not far from hence the first promulgators of Christianity had a chapel; and it is supposed, this part of Scotland was the first which received those doctrines now so widely diffused.

What religion prevailed here since that period is not easy to determine, for even the Songs of the Bards do not throw any light upon this matter. I imagine the Druidical Worship was never established in this country; for, though the vestiges of that worship are frequently found in ENGLAND and WALES, nothing of the kind is to be met with here: I am informed, that towards the western Highlands there are some Druidical temples, but of this I am not certain.

The Town of St. ANDREW's is respectable on many accounts, and abounds with antiquities: I can assure you I feel great pleasure in being a Burgess; and it was with regret I took my leave, after having amused myself for some time with the Gentlemen GOLFERS, at their diversion.

On Sunday last about eleven o'clock at night I reached Edinburgh, where, for about a couple of hours, I regaled my mind with reading the great number of Letters, Cards of congratulation, Compliments and Invitations which had been left at my Lodgings.

My first visits were to those Gentlemen, who, as I have already related, had interested themselves in behalf of my undertaking: they now expressed the most sincere and heart-felt satisfaction for my success, and felicitated themselves on their exertions in my favour. The two following days I had the honour of being visited, in my own appartments, by a great number of Gentlemen; and, as I walked through the streets, was attended by many hundreds of people, who viewed me with silent Astonishment!

A report had been circulated that the expence of my new apparatus would entirely deprive me of any profits arising from my experiment and exhibition; in consequence of which, my good friends, without acquainting me, had opened a subscription to make up the deficiency. As a further instance of liberality, I send you the copy of a letter which I received,

in

in anfwer to my propofal of afcending for the benefit of the *Charity Work-houfe.*

" To VINCENT LUNARDI, Esq;

" SIR, *Edinburgh.*

" THE Managers of the Charity Work-houfe re-
" ceived, by Sir William Forbes, your generous of-
" fer of exhibiting an afcent in your Balloon for the
" benefit of the Public Charity of this City, and
" they fincerely return you thanks, in the name of
" the community, for your benevolent intention.

" At a meeting of the Managers, called this day
" in confequence of your offer, they were unani-
" moufly of opinion, that, however much they were
" inclined to ferve the caufe of the indigent and un-
" fortunate, yet they could not think of any indivi-
" dual rifking his life for fuch a purpofe.

" If any thing adverfe fhould happen, they could
" not fail to be greatly diftreffed, and their conduct
" might be blamed by their fellow citizens.

" They are of opinion, that your fortitude and
" magnanimity, in exhibiting fo new, hazardous, and
" expenfive an experiment, fhould be amply re-
" warded by the public; and the emoluments that
" can be derived will be but a poor compenfation.

" They heartily wifh you all fuccefs: And I am,
" for the Managers,

" Sir,

" Your humble fervant

" WILLIAM CREECH, Prefes."

On Wednesday last I was made a Member of the ROYAL ARCHERS COMPANY; and on the Thursday following, had the wished for honour of being presented with the Freedom of the Metropolis by the LORD PROVOST and MAGISTRATES; on both these occasions I was most splendidly entertained: in short, it is impossible to express in adequate terms, the favours which have been heaped upon me, or my sensations of gratitude: The latter you will most easily conceive, as your instructions alone have served to imprint them upon my heart, whence no power can ever erase them! Were it possible to do that, the politeness and attention of the SCOTS might tempt me to forget my friends in ENGLAND; but reason, sentiment, and the involuntary impulse of the soul, call aloud for an equal division of my acknowledgements, and bid me not be unmindful of past favours.

As the EDINBURGH BURGES TICKET may perhaps afford you some pleasure, I shall transcribe it, that you may be acquainted with the very great honour they do me in mentioning the occasion of my being presented with it.

"AT EDINBURGH,

" The Twelfth Day of October, One Thousand
" Seven Hundred and Eighty-five
" Which day, the Right Hon. *James Hunter Blair*
" Lord Provost, James Dickson, James Gordon,
" Thomas Sanderson, and George Schaw, Esquires,
" Bailies, William Galloway, Esq. Dean of Guild,
" and

" and James Eyre, Efq. Treafurer, all of the City of
" Edinburgh, in Common Council Affembled: In
" Teftimony of their Senfe of the undaunted Courage
" of Vincent Lunardi, Efq. of Lucca, in Afcending in
" a Balloon, and paffing the Frith of Forth to Fife
" with the Wind at *South Weft*, at the manifeft rifk
" of being Blown into the German Ocean, Admitted
" and Received and hereby Admit and Receive him a
" Burges and Guild Brother of the faid City. Extracted
" forth of the Council Records of the faid City,

    " By Jos. WILLIAMSON."

Enclofed you have the copy of a Letter written by the Gentleman who faw me defcend at CERES; it will enable you to form fome idea both of the qualities of his head and heart, as well as his feelings on this occafion; I tranfmit this with the more pleafure, becaufe he has already publifhed it in the newfpaper.

Adieu! my revered friend; I fear to weary your patience with fuch unmerciful long letters; but, when thus converfing with you, unlefs the intruder bufinefs commands my attention, I cannot quit my pen till I have informed you of every circumftance that touches, and every thought that rifes in the foul of

    Your

    V. LUNARDI.

Copy of the Rev. Mr. ARNOT'S LETTER.

To the Printer of the Edinburgh Evening Courant.

SIR,   *Manse of* CERES, 6*th Oct.* 1785.

" THE following account of Mr. Lunardi's defcent near this place, will, perhaps, contribute a little towards gratifying the curiofity of the public, and may not be unacceptable to your readers.

" Yefterday afternoon the fky being clear, and a gentle breeze blowing from S. S. W. whilft I was overlooking the ftacking of fome corns in my barn-yard, a boy, who was ftanding by me, took notice of what he thought to be a hawk foaring at a very great and uncommon height. After looking attentively at the object, which appeared due fouth from me, and evidently higher than fome thin clouds which were floating near it, I was convinced it was no bird. At this time, which was about five minutes before four o'clock, it had the appearance of a globe or ball of fix inches diameter, and feemed fufpended without motion: This was owing to its furprifing and almoft incredible degree of elevation, and to its moving directly towards me. As I knew Mr. Lunardi was to afcend at Edinburgh on Wednefday the 5th inftant, and as the wind blew directly from Edinburgh towards Ceres, I was perfuaded that the object which prefented itfelf to view was Mr. Lunardi's Balloon. I then called upon my neighbours and acquaintances to come and fee the aerial traveller; they thought me in joke, but upon my affuring them that I was ferious, they came out and faw the object which I pointed out to them, but could not bring themfelves to believe it was Mr. Lunardi. Whilft we gazed, the intervening clouds two or three times intercepted our view; and, as the Balloon came out from behind the clouds, the rays of the fun reflected from the weft fide of it, gave it the appearance of the moon feen by day light, five or fix days after the change.

"About ten minutes after four the Balloon began to defcend, and got below the clouds; it now affumed an oblong figure, and appeared much larger: The bafket and flag alfo became vifible. Multitudes now got fight of it, and the whole country was alarmed. As it drew near the earth, and failed along with a kind of awful grandeur and majefty, the fight gave much pleafure to fuch as knew what it was, but terribly alarmed fuch as were unacquainted with the nature of this celeftial vehicle, if I may ufe the phrafe.

"About twenty minutes after four Mr Lunardi caft out his anchor, and the Balloon refted near the Coal town of Callinge, on the eftate of the Hon. John Hope, Efq; a mile eaft from Ceres, and between two and three miles fouth eaft of Cuper in Fife. Mr. Robert Chriftie, fener of Callinge, happened to be near the place, and he immediately came up to him, enquired after his fafety, and affifted him in getting of out the bafket and in fecuring the Balloon. A vaft multitude from every quarter foon affembled, and gazed with aftonifhment on the daring adventurer.

"Ten minutes after he had reached the ground, I came to the place, and gave directions to the people who were present to assist him in getting the Balloon emptied, and getting it with the netting, basket, and other apparatus, safely packed up and put into a cart: Every one gave his assistance cheerfully, and the whole machinery was conveyed away in safety.

"A great number of gentlemen from different places in the neighbourhood came quickly together, and seemed to vie with one another in the marks of attention and civility which they shewed Mr. Lunardi. They in a body attended him to Ceres, where he was received with the acclamations of a prodigious multitude, his flag being carried in procession before him, and the church bell ringing in honour of such a visitant. After drinking a few glasses of wine at the Manse, and receiving there, and also in the house of Mr. Melvill, the compliments of a great number of Ladies and Gentlemen, he set out for Cupar about seven o'clock, in consequence of an invitation from the Lord Provost and Magistrates of that town, where he was received with the ringing of bells and the acclamations of thousands.

"Mr Lunardi gives the following account of his voyage: He ascended at Edinburgh, a little before three o'clock afternoon: the Balloon after rising took a north-east direction, and near to the island of Inchkeith came down almost to the sea; he then threw out some ballast, and the Balloon rose higher than before; a current of wind from the west carried him east near to North Berwick; a different current then changed his course and brought him over between Leven and Largo; after this a south-west breeze brought him to the place where he descended.

"When

" When the Balloon was at its higheſt elevation, the barometer ſtood at 18 inches $\frac{5}{10}$. Mr. Lunardi at this time found no difficulty in reſpiration. He paſſed through ſeveral clouds of ſnow, and loſt ſight at times both of ſea and land. The thermometer was below the freezing point, and he found himſelf very cold from the chilly air which ſurrounded him. His excurſion took up about an hour and an half; and it would appear he paſſed over upwards of forty miles of ſea, and about ten of land. This aerial voyage, the firſt that has been made in Scotland, is much talked of, and will be long remembered in this place: It is propoſed to diſtinguiſh, by ſome laſting monument, the place on which Mr. Lunardi alighted.

" This day Mr. Lunardi, with ſeveral gentlemen who attended him on the night of his arrival, was elegantly entertained at dinner by the Provoſt and Magiſtrates of Cupar, and afterwards preſented with the freedom of the burgh. In the evening he ſet out for Melvill houſe, the ſeat of the Right Hon. the Earl of Leven; and to-morrow he intends to viſit the ancient city of St. Andrew's.

I am, &c.

ROBERT ARNOT."

LETTER X.

Edinburgh, Oct. 11. 1785.

DEAR SIR,

I AM juſt now favoured with a Letter and Deploma from Sir JAMES LUMSDAINE, conſtituting me a member of a very reſpectable Society, called *Knights Companions* of the *Beggar's Benniſon* : and I am the more elated with this new honour, as I underſtand that my Patron the PRINCE of WALES had the ſame conferred upon him a few months ago. I cannot now explain to you the enigmatical meaning of the Beggar's Benniſon, but ſhall endeavour to do it *ad aures* : the following tranſcripts muſt gratify your curioſity for the preſent.

To VINCENT LUNARDI, ESQ.

At WALKER's HOTEL, EDINBURGH.

SIR,

" AS it ſeems to be ſet in for fine weather, I hope to ſee you in Fife to-morrow : But in caſe I ſhould not again have that pleaſure, I have admitted you a *Knight Companion* of the moſt *ancient* and *puiſſant order* of the *Beggar's Benniſon,* and with this have ſent you your diploma.

" CAPTAIN ERSKINE and my Brother, MAJOR LUMSDAINE, make offer of beſt compliments to you

" That

" That the Beggar's Bennifon may ever attend fuch bold adventurers, is the fincere wifh of

Sir,

Your moft humble fervant

Jas. Lumsdaine."

" *Innergellie near Anſtruther*,
  10*th October* 1785."

" P. S. I fhall be glad to hear you have received this. J. L."

Diploma of the Beggar's Bennison,

Jas. Lumsdaine, Prefes.

" By the Supreminently Beneficent, and Superlatively Benevolent Sir James Lumfdaine of Innergellie, *Sovereign* of the moft Ancient and moft Puiffant Order of the Beggar's Bennifon, and Merryland, in the Thirteenth Year of his Guardianfhip, and in that of the Order 5785.

" Having nothing more fincerely at heart, than the happinefs and profperity of our well-beloved fubjects, the inhabitants of our celebrated territories of Merryland, and the encouraging of trade, manufacturies, and agriculture in that *delightful* Colony : And whereas, We are fully fatisfied, That *Vincent Lunardi armigerum lucænfis*, has all manner of Inclination, as well as fufficient Abilities, and other neceffary Qualifications, for promoting thefe noble and laudable purpofes, and willing

willing that such bold Adventurers should have all suitable encouragement; We, do hereby create, admit, and receive him a Knight Companion of the most ancient and most puissant Order of the Beggar's Bennison and Merryland, by the name, stile, and title of Sir Vincent Lunardi, to be used and enjoyed by him in all time coming; with our full powers and priviledges of *ingress*, *egress*, and *regress*, from and to, and to and from all the harbours, havens, creeks, and commodious inlets upon the coasts of our said extensive territories at his pleasure, and that without payment of toll, custom, or any other taxes or impositions whatsoever.

" Done at the *Beggar's Bennison Chambers* of ANSTRUTHER, upon this tenth day of the month, known to the vulgar by the name of October.

" Witness, I the Recorder,

" P. PLENDERLEITH, D.R."

I shall set out almost immediately for KELSO; it is now the time of the Races, and I am invited thither by the CALEDONIAN HUNTERS. I have sent my apparatus before me, and, if no accident intervenes, my next shall inform you of another excursion; and, consequently, of an addition to the pleasures which, in this happy country, continually circulate round me, and bring a thousand reasonable joys to the heart of

Your affectionate

V. LUNARDI.

LETTER XI.

Kelso, October 20, 1785.

MY HONOURED FRIEND.

I DID not propose to write again till I had ascended from KELSO; but time tempts me with a few leisure moments, and I am thoroughly convinced that I cannot employ them better than in corresponding with my worthy Guardian.

I have now been four days here, three of which I have past in preparing for my aerial voyage, and every thing being in readiness last night, I went this morning, in high spirits, to amuse myself at the race ground.

The weather was fine and the concourse of people very considerable; the box was crowded with the most respectable company, but the number of ladies was less than I expected.

The races afforded me much entertainment, for though but few horses entered, they were very swift, and the riders excellent.

My attention however was more strongly fixed upon a match between the *Duke* of HAMILTON and ROBERT BAIRD, Esq; both of whom rode their own horses. Never did I behold a more admirable spectacle! My ideas rolling back through the wide channel of history, reverted to the GRECIAN STATES in the meridian of their glory: Methought I saw *two heroes* contending for the prize in the *Olympic Games*! Starting from the barrier they skimmed lightly over the

plain

plain hailed by an univerfal burft of applaufe! equally rapid the two courfers moved as if both were animated and directed by the fame fpirit. Expectation fixed the croud awhile in filence; but foon the murmurs began to rife: at firft, gentle as the founds from a well regulated hive of bees, they feemed but to float on the wind, by degrees the noifes encreafed; and now the fhouts of admiration and encouragement, the loud articulations of hope, the exclamations of joy, clamours of fufpenfe rent the very air! A few moments were likely to determine the victory; the *Duke* and his *Antagonift* exerted their utmoft efforts; their horfes flew, and fcarce appeared to touch the earth. Every eye was fixed upon them, and every heart panted as agitated in favour of one or the other of thefe eager competitors. The *goal* was in view; they darted forward with the velocity of lightning, and both reached it at the fame inftant, without the leaft perceptible difference! The race was ftill undecided; the palm of glory was not yet awarded. They ftarted again; again the fame applaufe, the fame emotions took place: every one was anxious to fee the termination of a conteft fo nobly purfued; once more they touched the *goal* at Mossa, and now only differed by the breaft of one of the animals.

I cannot exprefs the pleafure I took in this fight! more efpecially as it was to me quite new and furprizing, as you know, in Italy, people of rank never fhew themfelves to the public in fuch a confpicuous manner: frankly fpeaking, I own I highly approve this cuftom, becaufe it muft in a fhort time caufe the gentlemen of diftinction to excel in horfemanfhip.

The

The races here are supported by subscription; the GENTLEMEN bring LADIES along with them, they all dine together; after which the *latter* retire to dress, and are the first to enter the BALL-ROOM, whither they are soon followed by the GENTLEMEN. It is not uncommon, in this small country town, to find, in the evening, a most brilliant and numerous assembly.

The happiness I here enjoy does not proceed merely from the civilities and attentions hourly shewn me, but from the many opportunities of observing manners and customs calculated to preserve the peace and welfare, and heighten the pleasures of a social and deserving people: There is but one reflection to damp my joys, you are not here to share them with

The too fortunate

VINCENT LUNARDI.

P. S. My next shall, I hope, give you the particulars of my Aeriel Journey, of which you need be under no apprehension as this is an inland town.

LETTER XII.

My dear guardian,   *Edinburgh.*

ON my return to KELSO I instantly wrote down the particulars of my voyage, intending to transmit them to you without loss of time; I was however prevented by the impatience of the people there, who handed them from one to another till at last they got into the public *News-paper*. That I may gratify my wishes therefore, in making known to you the circumstances of my journey as speedily as possible, I shall, without ceremony, insert what appeared in the *Kelso paper*, which you may credit as every way authentic.

KELSO.

" Last Friday being the day appointed for Mr. Lunardi to ascend from the Church-yard here, about 11 o'clock forenoon two cannon were fired to give notice that he had begun to fill the balloon, the process of which succeeded to admiration. At half past twelve two guns were fired as a signal that the balloon could support itself. At one o'clock other two guns were fired, as a signal for the attendance of the ladies and gentlemen, as his departure was approaching. A quarter before two o'clock, the balloon being sufficiently inflated, he attached the car to it, and put therein a basket full of provision, four bags of dry sand for ballast, a grapple, several small ropes, a barometer, thermometer, compass, quadrant, &c. He then got into the car himself, and ordered the balloon to be carried into the middle of the Church-yard, and giving the fignal for two guns to be fired, he rofe perpendicularly from thence, at two o'clock precifely, in a grand and moſt majeſtic manner. Immediately on the rifing of the balloon, Mr. Lunardi ſtood up in the car, took off his hat and bowed to the fpectators. At a greater height, he threw out his flag, which is 48 fquare feet, and was faſtened to the car by a cord of 150 feet in length. About ten minutes paſt two, he entered a thin cloud, which pretty much obfcured the balloon, but he foon came out of it. At 21 minutes paſt two he entered another cloud, in which we loſt fight of him about four minutes, but the flag was ſtill difcernible below the cloud. When he again became vifible, he was feen going below all the clouds horizontally to the eaſt. About 50 minutes paſt two, he was loſt to the naked eye though feveral with glaſſes fay they faw him longer.

To thofe who were not prefent, it is impoſſible to give any idea of the beauty and grandeur of the fpectacle, which could only be exceeded by the cool and intrepid manner in which the adventurer conducted himfelf; and indeed he appeared more at his eafe than the greater part of the fpectators. The multitude aſſembled was very great, but had the day of his afcenfion been generally known in the country, we doubt much if the Church-yard, large as it is, could have contained all that would have been aſſembled on the occafion. So anxious were all ranks to be prefent, that, although it was market-day, moſt of the ſhops were ſhut by one o'clock.

The balloon, which contained about 500 yards of taffety filk, was ſhaped like a pear, 33 feet high, and

23 in diameter, with a netting over it, and striped with different colours. The car had a bottom of thin board, with a small netting round it, ornamented at the top with pink silk, fringed with gold lace. Mr. Lunardi was dressed in scarlet.

Mr. Lunardi has favoured us with the following particulars of his voyage, which is the second that has been performed in Scotland:

" As soon as he got up, he could plainly perceive the sea, and that his course was towards it. Twenty minutes after his ascending with his balloon, he got into a cloud, and lost sight of the earth; he might have gone through it to enjoy the higher region, where there is always a fine clear sky, but thought proper to keep himself down, to give pleasure to the spectators. At 25 minutes past two, he was only 4000 feet above the surface of the earth; he then observing the sea to be about 10 miles from him, he began to ascend higher, and when at the height of 6000 feet, the west wind above was stronger than below. He went through the cloud, and for two minutes observed the clearness of the sky above, and the thickness of the clouds beneath: his intention was to go in search of another current of air, but having no signals above for it, and being so near the sea, he thought proper to come in sight of the earth again, which he effected in 3 minutes. At three o'clock precisely, he was no higher than 3000 feet from the surface of the earth, and went horizontally at that height for five minutes; he then began to descend, as he thought the sea to be no more than a mile from him. At 20 minutes after three, he anchored

anchored on Doddington Moor, about four miles north-east of Wooler, where several country people were collected, but they were afraid to approach him: he called to them, and after repeated entreaties, they at length came up to him. Mr. Lunardi then enquired how far he was from the sea, and they told him four miles. Here Mr. Strother Ancrum, who had followed him on horseback for two miles, came up and shook hands with him. He desired six of the country people to draw him with the ropes to Berwick, but after having carried him about two miles, the wind blowing fresher, and in an opposite direction, the men were not able to hold the balloon. He came down in a field at Baremoor, where he emptied the balloon, with the assistance of the people, who were coming from every quarter. When Mr. Lunardi alighted, he had 60lbs. of ballast remaining, which made him regret much his not being able to proceed father on account of the sea being so near."

" Amongst the people who came to congratulate his safe descent, Mr. Lunardi took much notice of the two Miss Halls of Thornton, Miss Wilkie of Doddington, and Miss Car of Newcastle.—He gives much praise to Mr. Richard Thompson of Baremoor, who, after giving Mr. Lunardi every assistance in his power, ordered the balloon to be carried to his house, and politely insisted on Mr. Lunardi accepting of his horse home. Mr. Lunardi spent the night at Mr. Thompson's house, where he was entertained in the most hospitable manner, and after breakfast set off for Kelso, where he arrived on Saturday at one o'clock afternoon. He was met upon the bridge by a great number of the

town's

town's people, and rode in triumph to the Crofs Keys Inn, with his flag difplayed on the top of the chaife, the bells ringing, drums beating, and the people huzzaing, to welcome him on his arrival.

" On Saturday he dined with Sir James Douglas, and fupped with the gentlemen of the Caledonian Hunt. On Sunday he was entertained by Sir James Pringle at Stitchill, on Monday by Lord Home at Hirfel, and on Monday evening by our Antient Lodge of Free Mafons, of which he was admitted a Member. On Tuefday about noon he fet off for Einburgh.

Mr Lunardi's courfe was due eaft (till the end, when he was carried a little to the fouth) continued an hour and 20 minutes, travelled 25 miles, his higheft elevation, when above all the clouds, was 7700 feet.

About two hours ago I reached EDINBURGH in good health, and could not permit the poft to depart without acquainting you with the whole tranfaction. In my lodging I found feveral letters; in particular two from the moft refpectable people in GLASGOW; inviting me thither: I muft therefore pay a vifit to that CITY as foon as poffible; and I hope, in a few days, to write you from thence, and affure you once more how much I am, and ever fhall be

Your obliged and grateful

V. LUNARDI.

LET-

LETTER XIII.

My dearest Friend, *Glasgow.*

I AM already as well known in this City, as if I had refided in it fome months. About feven o'clock in the evening I arrived here, and was immediately favoured with the vifits of feveral Gentlemen who had been witneffes to my afcent from Edinburgh. As I paffed through the ftreets in the morning, a thoufand eyes were fixed upon me, and if I remained in view for any confiderable fpace, I had the pleafure of feeing the windows filled with eager beholders.

My firft vifit was to the chief Magiftrate, who received me with the greateft civility, and feems a mighty honeft, worthy, and well-meaning Gentleman. I lodge at the Tontine Hotel, adjoining to which is the moft elegant Coffee-Room I have feen in Europe. The City of Glasgow is in general very neat: the ftreets broad, well paved, and interfecting each other at right angles, give it a far more regular appearance than the Metropolis. The people apply themfelves, with unceafing induftry, to commerce and manufactures, which are carried to fuch an extent as to make Glasgow juftly reckoned the *richeft city* in Scotland. I could not help alfo remarking the great friendfhip and hofpitality which fubfifts in this part of Caledonia; the inhabitants not only vifit each other frequently at their own houfes, but each fhop has fuch a communication with its neighbour, that every commercial tranfaction is prefently known through the whole city; and hence any merchant is able to direct one, with certainty, where to find a piece of goods though he may not have it in his own fhop.

A few days after my arrival I became acquainted with one Mr. INGRAM, who feems very much interefted in my behalf, and by him I was introduced to Mr. FRENCH, a merchant of this place, uncommonly popular for his generofity and oppenefs of heart; he was formerly Provoft of the City, and though another is now invefted with that dignity, he ftill retains the title of Provoft FRENCH.

The UNIVERSITY of GLASGOW is one of the moft compleat that can be imagined, well calculated for diffufing every Branch of Science, and they have an excellent Obfervatory charmingly fituated in their extenfive garden.

As this garden feemed to me the moft eligible place for my afcent, I applied to the Profeffors for it; but they in a polite manner declined granting my requeft, on account of many young trees which might be injured by the concourfe of people: I was therefore advifed to open a fubfcription for defraying the expence; which accordingly was done three days fince, but it goes on flowly.

I have had many rambles through the city, but can find no place that will anfwer my purpofe: I do not like to run the hazard of lofing a *confiderable fum*; but, on the other hand, I am treated with fo much cordiality and civility, that I know not how to refolve, fo as at once to clear my heart and head from any
difgraceful

disgraceful reflections; but I am fully bent to acquaint you in my next with the final determination of

Your

VINCENT LUNARDI.

LETTER XIV.

Glasgow, November 22. 1785.

My Honoured Friend,

EVERY thing is settled and ready for my excursion; and, if the weather proves favourable, I shall go up to-morrow.

The day after my last was written, I went to St. Andrew's Church-yard, which indeed may be overlooked in every part, but the avenues are remarkably well fenced; for which reason I thought it would be convenient, for all those who had purchased tickets: I instantly applied to the Magistrates who very readily allowed me the use of it; in consequence of which, I advertized that, without waiting for the subscription, I intended certainly to ascend on Wednesday, trusting that the Ladies and Gentlemen of Glasgow would not permit me to be a loser by my ascension: and indeed I am already convinced that will not be the case, as I have been informed that, if the money arising from the exhibition shall prove deficient, they will immediately make up what is wanting;

ing; and I know that, in the courfe of this day, tickets to the amount of fifty Guineas have been difpofed of.

By the defire of many principal inhabitants I have exhibited my Balloon in the Old Church Choir, where, it was no fooner inflated, than fuch a crowd of people affembled as I do not ever remember to have feen in a place of the kind before : fo that, one way or other, money enough will moft probably be collected.

I have alfo the pleafure to inform you, that in confequence of an application to COLONEL FERGUSON, Commander of the 27th Regt. accompanied with a card from the Magiftracy, I fhall be attended by a good number of foldiers; and during the procefs of filling the Balloon, the Band of the Regiment will entertain the company with martial mufic.

By a perufal of all my Letters, you will find that my fpirits have in general been raifed and depreffed alternately : Nothing, however, has been able to conquer my refolution, and I have fo often fhewen myfelf fuperior to *Misfortune*, that I think fhe is by this time tired of perfecuting me; therefore I fubfcribe myfelf as cool, collected, and happy as ever,

Your fincere friend

V. LUNARDI.

LETTER XV.

Glafgow, November 25, 1785.

Dear Sir,

SUCCESS has overpaid my expectations! I am returned to the Careffes of my furrounding friends; and, in token of gratitude, fhall make a fecond afcenfion on Monday next: You will imagine, that I ought now to be fufficiently acquainted with the air, and perhaps call this rage for flying *mere madnefs*; but give me leave to urge a child-hood proof, that whatever our ideas may be in the bud, they fhoot into habit; grow as we grow, and with our fouls expand, till they become abfolutely conftitutional. When quite a fchool Boy, I ufed to look with contempt upon the *creeping worm,* or *fhard-borne beetle*; while my eyes were fixed with rapture and admiration upon the *bufy bee* and *gilded dragon-fly*: I was not fond of *quadrupeds*; the tricks and gambols of the playful Squirrel, or the frolickfome careffes of the Spaniel, afforded me little or no amufement: but Birds were my delight! I could liften to their fongs with inexpreffible pleafure, and with the moft eager attention, furvey their rapid flight through the air; they were objects of my LOVE and ENVY: Is it then to be wondered, that I court their company and emulate their mode of living?

Previous to the detail of my very fuccefsful expedition, I fhall infert a paragraph from the newfpaper, the publifher of which muft be a perfon who under-

(68)

ſtands ſomething of AEROSTATION, as he deſcribes my apparatus better than any other writer that has attempted the ſubject.

AN AUTHENTIC

ACCOUNT

OF

Mr. LUNARDI's AERIAL EXCURSION

From *St. Andrew's Church-Yard*, GLASGOW, on *Wedneſday the 23d inſtant.*

Extracted from the GLASGOW ADVERTISER, *November* 28, 1785.

ON Wedneſday laſt Mr. Lunardi fulfilled his promiſe in aſcending in his aerial Car from this city. He came to the place appointed at eleven o'clock forenoon, in company with the Officers of the 27th Regt. preceded by the Muſical Band, and followed by all the ſoldiers under arms. After they had taken their ſtations at proper places, every thing was got ready for beginniug the operation about twelve. The Balloon was ſuſpended at the eaſt end of St. Andrew's Church, by a rope ſtretched between the top of the Church and the ground at ſome diſtance. Three very large caſks with iron hoops were ſunk to ſome depth in the ground, for the purpoſe of containing the oil of vitriol and iron neceſſary for the operation. Theſe caſks were furniſhed with large tin tubes, which, paſſing through a large veſſel of water to cool the vapour, united into one, round which the mouth of the Balloon was tied. Upwards of a tun weight of iron ſhavings were divided among the caſks, and five or ſix tuns of water along with them. A large tub lined with lead in the under part, with a hole in the bottom, was uſed as a funnel. This hole was cloſely ſtopt up with a ſtick, until the quantity of oil of vitriol deſtined for each caſk was put into it; when, by pulling out the ſtick, the whole quantity ruſhed in at once. There was ſixteen large bottles of oil of vitriol uſed, in all containing upwards of 2000 pounds. On mixing ſuch a quantity of hetrogeneous ſubſtances together, a tumult, effervescence, and heat, were inſtantly generated to ſuch a degree as cannot be conceived by thoſe who have not been eye witneſſes of ſimilar operations. The vapour inſtantly iſſued out with great velocity, and aſcending in the Balloon, began to ſwell it firſt at the top, ſo it became quite round and full there, while the under part remained quite flacid. By degrees the ſwelling proceeded downwards, and the net with which the Balloon was covered began to embrace it cloſely. About half an hour after twelve it was inflated ſufficiently to carry its own weight, ſo that the rope by which it was ſuſpended became no longer neceſſary, and was therefore taken away. The wind ſtruck one ſide of it confiderably, which rendering the operation of filling ſomewhat difficult, it was pulled down by means of the net and cords affixed to it, as cloſe to the ground

ground as poffible, which removed that difficulty. It was kept in this poffition till about half an hour after one, and though the fmell indicated fome lofs of inflammable air, yet confidering the large fcale on which the operation was conducted, we cannot help thinking that the chemical part was performed with great dexterity.

"As the Balloon now began to pull very ftrongly upwards, it was no longer confined, but gradually fuffered to rife to its full length, when it appeared of a beautiful oval fhape, but ftill fomewhat flaccid in the under part. The Car being now appended, Mr. Lunardi took his place, dreft in his regimentals, amidft the anxious expectations of the fpectators. At a quarter before two the Balloon, now floating with Mr. Lunardi in it, was conducted to fome diftance from the church, in order to give a more full view of his afcent. It was then let go, and began to rife fomewhat flowly; but Mr. Lunardi foon quickened it by throwing out a fand bag, and as its afcending power was not yet anfwerable to his wifhes, he in a few minutes threw out another, and after that a third. Thus the Balloon rofe with great rapidity, to the admiration of every one who faw it, and being impelled by a brifk gale, flew alfo with immenfe velocity in a S. E. direction as it afcended; and during this afcent Mr. Lunardi gradually lowered his flag to a confiderable diftance from the Balloon, which occafioned no little uneafinefs among the fpectators, many of whom immagined that the Car was getting loofe and falling away. In about a quarter of an hour our adventrous hero was loft in a cloud, to the great concern of the fpectators, and though a glimpfe or two of the Balloon

were

were afterwards obtained, it was impossible to view it distinctly for any length of time. He was seen passing over Hamilton at two o'clock, so that he must have been flying at the rate of forty miles an hour. The Magistrates, in testimoney of their esteem for Mr. Lunardi, ordered the bells to be set a-ringing; and in about ten minutes after he was seen passing over Lanark. In the course of his journey, it is said, he met with a southerly current, along with which he was carried for about twelve minutes, but afterwards returned into his former course.

It is impossible to describe the astonishment and admiration which Mr. Lunardi's ascent occasioned in this place. Indeed the sight of the Balloon, with Mr. Lunardi ascending along with it, was majestic and beautiful beyond description. To this indeed the gracefulness and genteel air of his person, with his easy intrepidity in the moment of ascent, contributed not a little. The most majestic part of the scene indeed was only visible to those in the Church-yard, being in a great measure lost by the rest of the spectators who did not purchase tickets. The concourse of people was amazing. The Green, the tops of the houses, and all places, where the sight could be had for nothing, were immensely crowded. Many were amazingly affected. Some shed tears, and some fainted; while others insisted that he was in compact with the Devil, and ought to be looked upon as a man reprobated by the Almighty.

" During the whole time that the Balloon was filling, Bailie Brown attended in the absence of the Lord Provost, and shewed the greatest attention to
Mr.

Mr. Lunardi; and invited the principal persons, who were strangers, to dine with him in the Tontine, among whom was the Earl of Loudoun; and an Assembly was held in the evening.

" While the Balloon was filling the company were entertained by the Musical Band of the 27th Regt. just now quartered here, who played a quick March as he went up. It is computed that there were upwards of 100,000 spectators assembled on this occasion, among whom were the greatest number of Ladies ever seen in Glasgow, who were all very much interested in Mr. Lunardi's safety. As no accounts of his landing arrived on Thursday, many people began to fear some fatal accident, but their apprehensions were happily dispelled on Friday by the following letter to Colonel Ferguson:

Edinburgh, Friday Morning, 11 *o'clock.*

" SIR,

" I have the honour to inform you, that at 42 minutes after three o'clock on Wednesday evening, I touched the ground upon high hills, where the wind being very fresh, the cable gave way, and I lost the great anchor and flag; the Balloon being then lighter ascended to a considerable height, and entirely lost sight of the earth. At 55 minutes after three I finally descended about two miles to the east of Alemoor on the water of Ale, in Selkirkshire, and luckily met with Mr. and Mrs. Chisholm, who were riding on the mountains in their way home from a visit; and the

Lady

Lady took my place (being lighter) in the Balloon, went three miles in it.

" Yesterday I was entertained by the Gentlemen of Hawick, and the Magistracy presented me with the freedom of the town.

" This morning I reached Edinburgh, and to-morrow at twelve o'clock at noon, I hope I shall have the honour to return you *viva voce* my sincere thanks, as I do with my pen, for all your kindness. I have the honour to be, &c.

Vincent Lunardi."

" According to his promise in this letter, Mr. Lunardi arrived with his Balloon in this city, about half an hour after twelve o'clock on Saturday; and was entertained at dinner by the principal merchants, and yesterday by the officers of the 27th Regt."

At five minutes before two, by my watch, I parted from the ground, but could not judge of the ascending power of the Balloon, by reason of its waving with the wind, which was pretty high. Being therefore apprehensive of its again descending to the ground, I threw out two bags of sand in the very church-yard, after which I ascended with great velocity, and saluted the very respectable and brilliant company whom I had left, and the multitude of spectators who were assembled all round, by lowering my flag about sixty feet from the bottom of the gallery

(74)

It was now exactly two o'clock, when I entered a very thick but small cloud; on which I pulled the valve in order to defcend below it, but the afcending power was too great, fo that I continued to rife for fome time longer.

On my coming again in fight of Glafgow, I found the compafs had fhifted $\frac{4}{36}$; the wind being N. W. I now paffed through higher clouds, and at five minutes after two, faw Hamilton about two miles diftant. The Balloon had now loft its rifing power, the rarefication of the air having expelled a great quantity out of it. I could fee Lanark very well, but it was foon intercepted by a fmall and thick cloud. Finding myfelf defcending, I threw out half a bag of fand; but that proving infufficient, I threw down the whole, on which the Balloon ftood motionlefs for about two minutes, and then began to afcend at a good rate. I entered a thick cloud about three quarters of a mile perpendicular, when I could neither fee heaven nor earth, being in fhort involved in an ocean of clouds, which about a mile above me I perceived were of different and beautiful colours.

While involved in thefe clouds, I dined, and having emptied one bottle of its contents by making a hole in its fide, as I could not uncork it. I threw it down altogether, and heard it whiftle as it defcended, for 35 feconds. The wind was now due fouth by the compas, and, being extremely fatigued and fleepy, having fcarce refted three hours the preceding night, I lay down in the bottom of the gallery. That I might not, however, incur any danger

by

by sleeping in this extraordinary situation, I fastened a small stillyard to a piece of rope, and this to the neck of the Balloon, so that it was suspended about a foot distance from my face. The Balloon was at this time keeping itself quite full by the rarefaction of air; and I was sure, that when it began to descend it must become flaccid, and consequently longer, so that the stillyard would hit my face and awake me. Without the least apprehension therefore I fell asleep, and enjoyed a comfortable nap for about twenty minutes, when the hook of the stillyard got hold of my chin, and I got up at once. I could now see the earth quite plain, and a serpentine river beneath me. I had no map, and the Balloon was turning upon its axis, so that I could form no judgment of my situation; but turning upon my right, I could perceive that the river below me was the Forth. It was then twelve minutes after three when I threw out half a bag of sand to keep me in a horizontal direction; and afterwards tried to descend on the other side of the river; but I saw with surprise that the Balloon was again approaching to the river, when I dropped my pocket book, and which appears to me has fallen about a mile to the north of Forth. The Balloon quickly crossed the river again, on which I threw away the remainder of the bag, but still the Balloon rose but very little, and was involved in thick clouds on my coming to the S. E.

At 25 minutes after three the earth began to appear, and I found I was over huge hills, which I judged to be the Highlands. Being now descending very quick, I threw down the rest of my ballast, and rose to a considerable height, but still in sight of the earth.

earth. At 38 minutes after three I was again descending, and faw the tops of the hills paffing very quick, by which I judged that the wind was very high. I intended to come down betwixt fome of thefe hills, as I could not fee the end of them, and fleep there all night; and with this view let loofe the big anchor about 60 feet from the gallery, and began to defcend: As foon as the anchor got hold of the ground the cabel gave way, and the anchor remaining in the ground, as well as the flag, &c. in all about 18 pounds weight, the Balloon rofe again with great rapidity; and when above all the clouds I could perceive that they had the very fame fhape of the hills below. The water generated by the inflammable air came down converted into icicles: I tafted a piece of it, and found it was fimilar to that of a long Scotch turn.p. I paffed horizontally through the clouds for about eight minutes: when I came in fight of the heathy hills again, I heard a voice call, " *Lunardi*, " *come down*," quite plain, and I knew not who it was;—I faw at a diftance fheep feeding, but could not fee a human being; and I was greately furprifed to hear my name pronounced by any fhepherd that might have been there with his fheep; and I could perceive no houfe, nor even huts in the neighbourhood. I called aloud feveral times through the hill and after one third of a minute, or 19 feconds, I could hear the echo of my words returned as loud as they were pronounced; but I never had repeated *Lunardi come down*, though I heard thefe words feveral times repeated, on which I anfwered through the trumpet, *Hallow, hallow*, with a great voice;—I heard the

words,

words, *Lunardi, hallow,* repeated; and being now quite free from any interruption from clouds, I could see distinctly some people on horseback;—at last I endeavoured to hasten my descent betwixt two hills where the Balloon might be sheltered from the high wind; and indeed I came down as light as a feather. Two trembling shepherds came to me, an old man and a boy, whom I encouraged by calling to them " My dear friends come hither." They crossed the water and came up to me, and I gave them some spunge bread that remained of my provissions; then a Gentleman came, asking how I did, and at what time I set off from Glasgow; after a proper answer, I reached him with the Balloon, and he mentioned the circumstances of meeting me as he was coming from a visit with his wife.

" I asked the Lady if she would get into the Balloon; who hardly had pronounced I will, when she got into the gallery, and I went out desiring the shepherds to hold the ropes; I got upon her horse, and in company with her husband we followed her. After three good miles riding, I saw that the Balloon was very much waved; and the shepherds carried by it at a great rate, so that I thought proper to call the Lady down, and it was with great difficulty and fatigue all of us together could succeed in emptying the Balloon, which I committed to the shepherds care, and went along with the Gentleman and Lady; at seven o'clock we arrived at their house at Stretches, where I was very well entertained. I had a comfortable sleep; and next morning after breakfast, the Gentleman

man in whose house I was, took me to Hawick, where I was received by the Gentlemen and the Magistrates, who very generously invited me to dinner with them, and presented me with the freedom of the town; soon after dinner, I got into a post chaise, travelled all night, and reached Edinburgh at six o'clock in the morning, when I wrote a letter to you with two inclosed, and dispatched by an express to Glasgow, as I knew they would have been in anxiety. My course was S. E. then N. and then S. E. the whole of my journey 110 miles; the descent and place will be better described by the Gentleman with whom I was so fortunate as to meet.

Extract of a Letter from Gilbert Chisholm, Esq; Stretches, to a friend in Glasgow, November 23.

" Yesterday afternoon, about half an hour after three, as I was returning, with Mrs. Chisholm, from a visit to Sir James Nasmyth of Posso, Bart. my servant called out to me to observe a paper kite of most surprising magnitude and height. Turning my eyes to the place where the boy pointed, I perceived a body flying among the clouds, which sometimes intercepted it from my sight. As it came near the ground I perceived it assume an oblong oval shape, somewhat like a sugar mould, but as I could perceive no string to hold it, nor any tail appended, I was convinced that it could be no kite, which indeed its extraordinary height had convinced me of before. As I knew that Mr. Lunardi was in the country, and intended a voyage from Glasgow this day, I began to suspect

suspect this must be his Balloon, though I was yet unable to distinguish his car, and could scarce allow myself to think that he could be at such a distance from that city. As it still came nearer, however, I was at last convinced that it could be no other; and in about a quarter of an hour after I first saw him, he was got so near that I began to call out to him " *Mr. Lunardi come down, come down!*" This invitation I gave him the more earnestly, because if he had still gone on, he must have alighted in a very inconvenient place on account of the high wind. After repeated calls, I had the good fortune to hear that he answered me through his speaking trumpet, though I could not distinctly hear what he said. At five minutes before four he alighted in a place very near the water of Ale, and so screened from the wind, that the Balloon stood quite upright without inclining either to one side or another. Two shepherds who kept their sheep on the hill side were so much astonished at the descent of the Balloon with a human creature appended to it, that it was with difficulty I could persuade them that Mr. Lunardi was not some Devil who would destroy them. At last by my earnest persuasion they ran down the hill and, with some signs of fear came up to Mr. Lunardi My horse was so much frightened that I could scarce come within a gunshot, but Mrs. Chisholm, who rode a more peaceable beast, was allowed to come much nearer. The shepherds at my desire conveyed the Balloon, and Mr. Lunardi along with it, over the water which separated us, which they effected with the greatest ease, the Balloon yet rising from the ground with the slightest touch.

touch. After receiving our hearty congratulations, Mr. Lunardi afked Mrs. Chifholm if fhe would take his place in the aerial car, to which fhe replied by jumping into it. She willingly would have had the Balloon fet at liberty, but as the wind was very high, Mr. Lunardi judged this to be improper; for, as Mrs. Chifholm is confiderably lighter, fhe muft have afcended to a great height, and been conveyed to feveral miles diftance. The car therefore held near the ground by the two fhepherds. In this manner fhe was carried for about three miles, while the hills fheltered us from the wind; but then it became fo violent, and the Balloon waved fo much, that fhe was obliged to alight. After this we affifted Mr. Lunardi in emptying his Balloon, which was not accomplifhed without great difficulty on account of the high wind. After having the pleafure of Mr. Lunardi's company for the night, I had the honour of introducing him this day to the Magiftrates of Hawick, who after having entertained him at dinner, prefented him with the freedom of the city.—Mrs. Chifholm is much pleafed with her aerial journey, and ftill wifhes that fhe had been fet at liberty. As the report of Mr. Lunardi's landing has already fpread to a confiderable diftance, our market of Hawick has been uncommonly thronged by multitudes of country people who have come to town in hopes of feeing this aerial hero."

I fhall

I shall not have occasion to write to you again till I have taken my second flight from this place, as I cannot suppose that any accident will impede my enterprise, the apparatus remaining as I left it. This evening I intend to advertise my pocket book, with two guineas reward to any person who may have found it; the original value is no more than twelve shillings, and it contains nothing but a paper of calculations and two letters, with my direction, one of which is your last, dated 26th October: My wishes are only to ascertain the place where it was found.

To-morrow I shall visit PAISLEY, where some beautiful manufactures are carried on. It is very astonishing that in FRANCE and ITALY, where such a quantity of silk is produced, this branch of business should not be carried into the same degree of perfection as here! On Sunday I propose to return, and Monday is the day fixed for my ascension; soon after which, if no unlucky accident intervenes, you shall again hear from

Your affectionate and respectful

V. LUNARDI.

LETTER XVI.

Glasgow.

MY EVER HONOURED FRIEND,

WITH additional pleasure I once more take up my pen to inform you of another aerial voyage. Happiness is doubly dear when thus communicated to a friend! What numberless blessings has the ART of WRITING diffused! How many remarkable events has it perpetuated! How many nations has it taught to imitate the virtues of their ancestors! Without this, the dearest friends, when separated by distant countries, would be as dead to each other: By means of this noble discovery, we communicate our inmost thoughts to, and receive the kind sentiments of those we love and esteem, while intervening oceans roll their rude waves in vain: but let me not, while I praise, misuse the blessing, by wasting time in idle reflections, which I am convinced will not be half so interesting to your heart as the following particulars of my late journey:

The auspicious morning being arrived, every thing was ready by ten o'clock for beginning the operation. Exactly at eleven, I was honoured with the attendance

ance of the 27th Regt. as on the former occasion, to support the Civil power in keeping the peace, and preserving regularity; though, thanks to God, no riot or disturbance ever happened at any of my experiments, the people being universally acquainted with my upright principles, and convinced of my intention to fulfil my promise in the most ample manner.

My two small casks, containing one half of the ingredients for filling the balloon were instantly set to work; but as, at half an hour after eleven, there were but very few people assembled, I was advised by several respectable friends not to go on with the other, until a greater number of spectators should arrive. The operation therefore went on but slowly, but at twelve, I ordered the large cask to be set to work: by which means the balloon was sufficiently inflated by half an hour after one.

During this process I could not help paying very particular attention to the different currents of wind, which indeed did alarm me very much. On this account I was obliged to decline the taking with me a young gentleman of this place, only twelve years of age, but of undaunted spirit, and who might have been a very agreeable companion to me, had the weather been mild; but the voyage at this time was very dangerous as I myself very soon experienced. For the same reason I was obliged with regret to refuse the request of Captain Barns of the 27th regiment, who had several times earnestly expressed to me his desire of taking an aerial voyage, and at this time wished to have gone in my place. The answer I gave him at present, however,

ever, was, "that I would not, on this day, send up any friend of mine for all the gold in the world."

The wind in the lower regions had all this time been shifting almost every five minutes; and in the space of an hour, had gone round three fourths of the compass. The currents above were evidently W. and S. W. and E. and S. E. To avoid any danger from the church, I ordered the balloon to be carried to the end of the railing, and there I fastened the gallery to it. The wind was high, and tossed the balloon excessively: however I got into it, having all the instruments and provisions I wanted, there already. I desired several officious gentlemen to let it go; but you cannot conceive, my dear friend, the attachment of every body here to me, how earnestly they wished to be near me, and offer me their services in the moment of ascension. I got up, however, about 50 feet from the ground, when the rope I had left loose for my servant to give me the rising power I wanted, when cleared of my friends below (which however proved impossible) entangled a gentleman, who, I since understand, is a minister; and, with the greatest concern, I saw him dragged for a considerable way along the ground, till the rope was cut by my servant.

It was now near 40 minutes after one o'clock, and my ascent was not very rapid; as I could see the people below for six minutes. This time I employed in securing the gallery to the balloon better than it had been done below; waving the flag, saluting the public. Soon after I lost sight of Glasgow. The wind below was S. E. and I took my course to N. W. so that I was kept in view by every body. At 48 minutes after one, I was obliged to secure the compass and watch, and take hold of the upper hoop with both my hands; as the gallery was not only waving, but all to one side. The balloon being preffed by two contrary winds, turned upon its axis at leaft twelve times in ten feconds, and jumped up to a great height. It was now quite full; the inflammable air efcaping very faft from the neck, and I opened the valve befides, when all at once it fell down for a quarter of a mile and there became ftationary; it was now two thirds full, and the filk below fticking together, and driven with the violence of the wind, made a terrible and hideous noife; keeping the valve conftantly open, fo that I could hear the inflammable air whiftle in efcaping.

At 52 minutes after one o'clock the balloon was prodigioufly inclined to one fide, and gallery almoft overturned, fo that I was exceedingly alarmed, being obliged to hold the upper hoop where the net terminated faft with both my hands. I then found myfelf attacked by two contrary winds; the balloon turned with great velocity upon its axis, and jumped up about 100 feet, then began to defcend with fuch rapidity that I could fee the clouds below approached me very faft, and fome paffing very rapidly. When the gallery began to keep itfelf fteady again, I endeavoured to put out both my anchors; the fmalleft faftened to a very long rope, and the biggeft to a fhorter one: I threw down two bottles I had full of water, and all the ballaft at once, which did indeed check the rapidity of my defcent, but could not give the balloon levity enough to rife again; the fmall anchor got hold of the earth, as well as the large one; I then fufpended myfelf to the upper part of the gallery, letting the bottom
of

of it receive the blow from the earth, which broke in two parts, and I got a very violent shock, but happily am not hurt. It was just two o'clock when I descended.—In the place where I alighted there was but very little wind, and the balloon stood perpendicular. Both the anchors having got hold of the ground, I could have come out of the car and done every thing myself without any assistance, but I was immediately surrounded by a great many, who were all very ready to offer me their service, and did as much as was in their power to assist me, and take care even of the smallest thing.

The Reverend Mr. Lapsley, the minister of the parish in which I descended, was the first gentleman who reached me, and he very politely sent his servant to take care of the balloon, &c. and expressed his joy in having accidentally met with such an extraordinary piece of good fortune in meeting me. While I was going towards his house, accompanied by the whole multitude of people collected on that spot, we saw at a distance, a gentleman advancing very fast: this was Sir Alexander Stirling; who invited me and the minister to his house, where we were well entertained. But it is beyond the power of my pen to paint to you the happiness of this old gentleman, in having me at his house, in such an extraordinary way, and his expressions on the occasion.

Mr. Lapsley agreeably amused me while at dinner with a conversation upon aerostatic experiments. He seems to be a very intelligent gentleman, and has written a letter to a friend of his in Glasgow, a copy of which I inclose for your inspection, and which will enable you to form some judgement of his sensibility.

At

At seven o'clock in the evening, a chaise being ready, I took leave of Sir Alexander, and was accompanied by Mr. Lapsley to Glasgow. I went immediately to the play, where I was received with great applause.

This day I was entertained at the Saracen's Head, with a very splendid dinner by Provost French, Mr. Ingram, and several of the best citizens, where I was presented with the diploma, and made KNIGHT of the CAPE. Indeed I am very much caressed through all Scotland, therefore if I be attached to this nation, you cannot think it any wonder.

I reckon it a very fortunate circumstance that in this descent, as well as a former one, I should meet with a *Minister* young, sensible, and accomplished; such is Mr. LAPSLEY: I shall transcribe a letter from him to one of his friends: his attention to the various occurences being more exact than what I could possibly pay, it has enabled him to observe, recollect, and mark down, the most minute circumstances.

Copy of a Letter from the Revd. JAMES LAPSLEY, *to a friend in Glasgow.*

DEAR SIR,   *Manse of Campsie, 6th Dec.*

Although you and my friends in Glasgow, have had the advantage in seeing Mr. Lunardi ascend twice into the atmosphere, I will not suffer you now to boast too much of your good fortune, for he has done me the honour of paying me a visit in my own parish. I saw him descend from his car: and was pleased with the remarks of the villagers upon his descent. The people of Campsie were too bold to be afraid of him: and they
are

are above difguifing what their feelings lead them to exprefs.

Yefterday afternoon whilft I was walking through my parifh, vifiting the fick, and rather inclined to be penfive from reflecting upon the fcenes of diftrefs to which I had been witnefs, my attention was fuddenly arrefted by a confufed humming noife, which feemed all at once to fpring out of the earth towards the fouth, but as my view from that quarter was intercepted by a clump of trees, I walked on, and for two minutes I had it not in my power to inquire from what caufe it proceeded.

An old woman at that moment joined me, hearing the noife at the fame time, took fome pains to convince me, that it was the buzz of thofe fpirits and elves who before Chriftmas Eve hold their meetings in fequeftered dales, lamenting their loft power.

You will eafily believe that fuch a wayward fancy was not then agreeable to my prefent humour. I left her, and haftened to a rifing ground, when I now heard diftinctly feveral people fhouting aloud, " Yonder he comes !" Turning round, I beheld the balloon failing majeftically almoft over my head. Mr. Lunardi was then ftanding in his car, and waving his banner. His diftance from the earth feemed to be about 400 yards. The people were coming from all quarters. Their acclamations were every moment waxing louder and louder; and the farmers, in imitation of Mr. Chifholm, were fhouting vehemently, " Lunardi come down." And I, along with the reft invited him to defcend.

I am

I am rather inclined, however, to think that he did not hear me, owing to the whistling of the wind, it being very violent during the whole of his excursion. However, as he had resolved not to go far, we were indulged in our request; for, exactly at two o'clock he descended at Easter Mockroft, on the banks of the Glassart on the estate of Sir Archibald Edmistone of Dultreath in the parish of Campsie, nine English miles and a half N. N. E. of Glasgow.

When I saw the balloon first, which was about two minutes and a half before two o'clock, it appeared to be very much agitated, turning round its axis, while it was floating through clouds of air, and the day being hazy, it resembled very much, in appearance, the full moon seen through a darkened glass labouring in an eclipse. Sometimes it appeared of an ash, sometimes of a copper colour; sometimes even darker; owing to the different shades reflected from the Campsie Fells. About half a minute however, before he alighted, the sun came out behind a cloud, and shone directly upon the balloon; every colour became distinctly seen; the various stripes of the flag became vivid; his regimentals and the decorations of the car affording a varied and most beautiful spectacle, according to the play of the different rays of the sun, and as my view on the north was bounded by the Campsie Fells, whose tops were then covered with blue mist, the balloon appeared, as it were, to come out of the mist, and descend in a sun beam.

As the balloon was perfectly unexpected by me, and as at the very first it appeared in all its grandeur, I confess, without hesitation, that the pleasure I had in seeing it sailing through the clouds, and descending in our sequestered vale, was a pleasure mixed with some degree of pain. I laboured, as it were, under the grandeur of the object, and strove to compare it to some thing I had seen; but I failed. However, a young gentleman happening to come up to me at that moment, whose imagination was not so overpowered, asked me if I thought it did not resemble the discription given by Milton:

> Nigh at hand hung high with di'monds flaming and with gold;
> Thither came Uriel gliding thro' the ev'n on a sun-beam,
> And swift as a shooting star which in Autumn thwarts the night.

I told the gentleman that this descrption was but a conceit in Milton, not ill pleased, however, to find that we had got some likeness, tho' fanciful, to compare it to.

As he had descended to within half a mile where I stood, I immediately hastened to welcome Mr. Lunardi, and to give him all the assistance in my power. The whole country seemed to be alive, running unto him with the same kind intention; and I perceived with pleasure, that curiosity was a principle not confined alone to the breasts of the higher born and better educated class of men; for, in passing a little cottage, I heard a weaver expressing the most vehement desire to see this great sight, and crying to his wife to "take care of the bairns." I believe, however, that she at this time forgot that ever she had promised him obedience, and set out, repeating his commands to the servant, who in her turn exclaimed with rage, that "she wondered what people imagined servants were "made of: Let those who got bairns take care of "them; for, by her faith, she would both see and "touch

"touch Lunardi with the beſt of them;" and threw the child from her. Perhaps upon another occaſion we might have taken time to tell her that ſhe expreſſed herſelf too ſtrongly; but yeſterday every thing was her friend.

During my going from the riſing ground where I firſt ſaw it to the vale where it alighted, I ſometimes loſt ſight of the car, by the gentle ſwells which intervened, but never loſt ſight of the Balloon; and as it was ſuſpended ſome yards from the ground, betwixt the darkneſs of the day, and the blue miſt of the mountains, under whoſe ſhade it was, it had the appearance of an object ariſing out of the ſea, reſembling the ſun when he makes his firſt appearance in a ſpring morning out of a thick fog. Before I arrived it aſſumed a new ſhape,—that of a pear, or inverted cone. Mr. Lunardi then ſtanding in his car, about four feet from the ground, ſome people aſſiſting him to get out, and others holding the rope in order to prevent him from being dragged along by the ſtrength of the Balloon, which was hovering above him.

It was about ſix minutes after two when I got up. More than forty people were before me. A vaſt multitude now aſſembled from every quarter. The ſhepherd forſook his flock, the farmer left his plow, and the traveller his journey, ſo that in leſs than a quarter of an hour there were many hundreds gazing with aſtoniſhment at the daring adventurer. Every body was pleaſed, and every body wiſhed to lend their aid. Mr. Lunardi hardly had occaſion to aſk for aſſiſtance, nor I to encourage them to give it. At half an hour after two the Balloon was emptied, and the netting, baſket,

basket, and other apparatus, packed up, and all ready to march off the field.

Persons from different parishes now wished each to have the honour of his going to their particular village; however, as I had asked him to do me the favour of taking some refreshment at the Manse of Campsie, my parishioners were not then to be gain said; and in a sort of triumph we began our journey, when Sir Alexander Stirling of Glorat, one of my principal heritors, came running up, welcoming Mr. Lunardi, and insisting on his going to Glorat; which invitation we accepted of, as being nearer than the Manse, and we set out for that Gentleman's house in the following order.

A little pretty boy carying the banner; next came Mr. Lunardi dressed in his regimentals attended by the Baronet and myself. We were followed by a stout fellow carrying the anchor, then by four youths supporting the car; and then by six stout men bearing the Balloon; escorted by a vast number of people of all denominations. We had not indeed the ringing of bells, but we were cheared by the hearty acclamations, and repeated huzzas of many hundreds of the villagers expressing their joy at the unexpected visit.

In going to the Baronet's we had to cross over the bridge of Glassart, where about thirty young blooming lasses had ranged themselves on each side to have a sight of this comely Adventurer. All of them appeared well pleased: there was one, however, not the least lovely of the number, whose sensibility led her to express herself more strongly than the rest: " How pretty he is! I wish I had been with him."

Mr.

Mr. Lunardi was too attentive to let flip an opportunity to fay a civil thing to our fair Countrywoman; he patted her cheek, whifpering, " My Angel, and fo " do I." Whatever things this young woman may be difpofed to forget, I will engage for it fhe will never forget the looks fhe received from her companions at that inftant; nor the fenfations fhe felt when her cheek was preffed by the hand of this bold Italian.

We had now arrived within a few hundred yards of the houfe of Glorat; we ftopped at a little hamlet pointing out fome profpects to our new vifitor; when I perceived an old woman, whofe frailties would not permit her to run with the multitude, eagerly looking at him. She firft examined his flag; then fhe touched his clothes, and his body; and having heard him fpeak, rubing her eyes, fhe faid, " I am fure there is nae " Glammary here, but oh, Sirs, its a fair pity he " fhould be a papift." She was immediately checked by an old gray headed man; who in the pride of his heart exclaimed, " Be he Papift, or be he Pagan, fair " fa' him, tho' a' the kirk were here, and Lord George " at their head, I would drink his health, and here's " to him." Then addreffing himfelf to me, " Oh, " Sir, I am an auld man, I am aulder than the Union, I " have feen mony things, but the like of this I never " faw. I have feen Marr's year, and the Highland-" men's Raid; and about twelve years fyne, I gaed " o'er by yonder (pointing to the Canal) to fee fhips " failing thro' dry land; but the like of this I never " faw. Dinna ye think the world will foon be at an " end."

" We

"We arrived at Glorat at three o'clock, where we dined; and having drank a few glaſſes of wine and coffee, a poſt chaiſe was got; and as I was obliged to come to Glaſgow that night upon buſineſs, I begged to accompany him. We ſet out from Glorat at half an hour after ſix, and arrived in Glaſgow a little before eight. Mr. Lunardi alighted at the Tontine amidſt the huzzas of a vaſt concourſe of people, who had aſſembled anxious to expreſs their joy at his arrival.

"Having promiſed his friends before he ſet out in his aerial excurſion that he would certainly if poſſible be at the play that night, he immediately therefore got dreſſed; went to the houſe about nine; and was again received by the acclamations of the young, the gay, and the fair.

"P. S. As I was obliged to leave the town without ſeeing you, I took the liberty of writing to you my obſervations on his deſcent, and the varied ſentiments of cutioſity and ſurpriſe which the ſpectators expreſſed: perhaps it may contribute to your amuſement in an idle hour."

To-morrow morning, about four o'clock, I ſhall ſet out for EDINBURGH, where I know they are all in expectation of ſeeing a ſecond excurſion; and if poſſible I mean to aſcend from HERRIOT's GARDEN, on Monday 19th inſtant.

Adieu!

Adieu! my honoured friend; give my best love to my dear sisters, and believe me to be, with the most sincere affection,

Truly your

V. LUNARDI.

LETTER XVII.

Edinburgh, December 11, 1785.

MY DEAREST FRIEND,

AT eleven o'clock this forenoon, I reached EDINBURGH, where, with other letters, I found two of yours, one dated the 2d, and the other the 7th November; I am truly sensible of the many obligations you have heaped upon our family: we all look upon you as a second father; and give me leave to pay my most grateful thanks for the kind part you have taken in my sister MARGARET's behalf! I know she would look upon your advice as that of an indulgent parent; but let me earnestly entreat, that you will not in any degree bias her inclinations. In an affair of such moment she cannot be too cautious; and I fear her prospects of happiness would be sadly clouded, should she marry a Gentleman whose advanced years must render him an unfit companion for a girl of three and twenty. Their tempers, their difpofitions, muft be widely different! AGE can ill accord with the lively fallies of YOUTH; or YOUTH accommodate itfelf to the gravity of AGE. I am proud to acknowledge the honour this match might reflect on our family; but, as MARGARET declares, fhe will act according to my advice, I beg you will tell her that, as a BROTHER and a FRIEND, I think that WEALTH, TITLES, and GRANDEUR, would be *poor, very poor* compenfations for the SACRIFICE of her AFFECTIONS.

In your fecond Letter I found enclofed one of introduction to your *old refpectable friend*; but I am extremely forry to acquaint you that his death was announced in an Edinburgh paper of the 16th November.

I propofe to afcend, on Monday the 19th inftant with two Balloons, the common one and another of ten feet diameter, which is already made, under my direction, by the girls of the MERCHANT'S HOSPITAL; it is to be 550 feet higher than that by which I am fupported, in order to afcertain the different currents of air.

The fame girls are alfo conftructing another Balloon which, though without any valve, is fo contrived as not to burft when the rarefaction of the air takes place, even though it fhould afcend with 100 pounds of rifing power; it is compofed of 100 yards of fine Perfian filk, in ftripes of pink, green, ftraw-colour, and white, and is defigned as a model of a large one which I mean to conftruct for a long journey.

Till

Till I return from my next flight, once more adieu, and believe me to be

sincerely yours,

V. LUNARDI.

LETTER XVIII.

Edinburgh, December 24, 1785.

MY REVERED GUARDIAN,

MY laſt Letter acquainted you that I propoſed aſcending with two Balloons; an experiment which however intereſting, I had not the good fortune to try.

The morning was tolerably favourable; but, as the day advanced, it became thick and foggy attended with ſmall rain: Senſible that under theſe circumſtances, I could not be viſible for more than two or three minutes, and that it muſt be very inconvenient for the LADIES to remain in an unſheltered place like that from which I was to aſcend, after ſome deliberation, I reſolved to delay the experiment to ſome more favourable day: At this time I obtained a promiſe from his Excellency GENERAL MACAY, that a gun ſhould be fired from the Caſtle at ten o'clock in the morning of that day, as a certain ſignal to the public;

lic : On which I immediately ordered hand bills to be distributed signifying my intentions.

In the afternoon I attempted to fill the small Balloon with a new apparatus, of my own invention, which succeeded beyond expectation! All this time, my large machine was kept inflated with atsmopherical air at the REGISTER OFFICE, where a vast concourse of people assembled, and some gentlemen, friends to my undertaking, staid to learn the opinions of the people in general respecting my conduct : I am happy to inform you, that *all* the LADIES approved it; and only a *very few Gentlemen* expressed their dissatisfaction; yet even this mark of disapprobation, trifling as it was, when reported to me, wrung my very heart, and I determined, if the weather proved tolerable, nothing should prevent my utmost efforts being exerted to ascend the day following.

On Tuesday, about seven o'clock, I arose, and perceiving it to be a fine morning, without noticing the direction of the wind, I ordered my servants to carry every thing necessary for my experiment to HERRIOT'S GARDEN, and wrote a note to the GOVERNOR of the Castle, begging to be favoured with the attendance of the Military and the firing of a gun, as had been promised : LORD ELPHINSTONE seemed greatly surprized at receiving such a card, as the wind was too much from the west, and therefore very obligingly sent me word, that he was ready to do every thing in his power for my service, but thought the undertaking too dangerous. My resolution, however, was unalterable; and his Lordship at last did me the

honour

honour to acquiesce in my wishes: on which I went to the Garden and prepared for my ascension.

A little after eleven o'clock I began to fill the Balloon, with half the apparatus, and in ten minutes it could support itself; but at this time there was not much company assembled. They said the gun was scarcely heard, and as the wind still continued westerly, people of sense could not imagine that I meant to venture. I now sent to GERERAL MACKAY, requesting the favour that another gun might be fired: this his Excellency readily granted; after which, the flag being hoisted on HERRIOT'S HOSPITAL, I set the remainder of the apparatus to work, and the number of spectators encreased very fast.

During the procefs I secured several bladders and pieces of cork round the car. The general question being "Whether I really intended to go up?" I made answer, that it was impossible to prevent my dropping into the sea, but I was confident some boat would arrive in time to my assistance.

Dressed in the uniform of the SCOTS ROYAL ARCHERS, five minutes before *one o'clock*, I rose majestically, though not with so great a degree of velocity as the former time. The wind was south-west. After saluting the spectators, I fastened some of the strings which had been left loose, and began to untwist the rope of the little anchor. In three minutes from the time of leaving the ground, I perceived myself perpendicularly over the FORTH.

Exactly at *one o'clock* the Balloon turned thrice round upon its axis, and was completely full; the barometer at 21; the thermometer at 38; wind S. W. by W.

by W. and I was moving very flowly, with the moft delightful Scenery beneath me!

Half after one, the Balloon continued much in the fame ftate; and the barometer had only fallen $\frac{2}{10}$: I was going horrizontally to the north-eaft, and faw a Boat rowing towards MUSSELBOURGH; I threw down a piece of cake, about half a pound weight; but do not know whether it fell into the boat.

Fifty minutes after one, the wind was due weft, and I therefore refolved to attempt landing on the POINT of ARCHER FIELD: For this purpofe I let go my fmall anchor, about 600 feet below my car, and began to defcend; but finding that I came down with too much rapidity, and had no ballaft nor the large anchor, I fhut the valve and threw down a bottle full of water, when about 2000 feet from the ground; by which means I paft over the Point of Land, and came again upon the Water. At this elevation the thermometer fell to 31. I faftened my Uniform Great Coat, my Hat, and fome other things to the upper Hoop, that they might not be injured by my falling into the Sea.

At five minutes after two I touched the Surface of the Water, not farther than a mile and a half from the rocks of FIDRA and LAMB: but, as the wind was pretty ftrong and the Balloon acted like a large fail upon my bafket, I made way very faft; the water dafhing againft me and fparkling like filver. I turned round and could fee no boat whatever; but, when about two miles and a half from the fouth fhore, could diftinguifh three fhips under fail near ANSTRUTHER or KILRENNY, and therefore was under no apprehenfions, prehenſions, as my courſe was towards them and the Island of May.

The Balloon was much agitated by the wind, and ſometimes turned round, ſo that I was frequently toaſſed into the water as high as my breaſt. When about five miles from North Berwick I perceived a black ſpot, appearing and diſappearing according to the riſing and falling of the waves, directing its courſe from the Bass: on paying more attention, I ſaw plainly that it was a Boat; but, as I was going with great rapidity, I quickly paſſed their Parallel, and then, as they had gained the wind and made uſe of their ſails as well as oars, I aſſured myſelf they would quickly reach me, and began to wave the flag as a ſignal that I had ſeen them.

The nearer I approached the ocean the wind grew briſker, and I began to be in doubt whether to cut away the Balloon or not; but, after mature deliberation, I reſolved to keep it; for, as darkneſs now began to draw nigh, I ſhould have been too ſmall an object without it to be viewed at any diſtance, being at this time *Breaſt-high* in the water.

As ſoon as the boat came up I threw out a ſtrong rope, deſiring the fishermen to make it faſt, but the moment I got on board they let it go and the Balloon was *inſtantaneouſly* out of ſight! And now my ſituation was not the moſt comfortable; heavy, with remaining ſo long in the water, my hands lacerated with clinging to the hoop, and every limb weared, I ſate down, as well as I was able, in a boat full of *fiſh*; while the ſharpneſs of the air contributed not a little to heighten my diſtreſs.

A

A King's boat soon came up, and the gentlemen very politely invited me on board; but I was obliged to decline this polite offer, that I might shew my gratitude to the people who had taken me up. I landed, on Archer-Field, about five o'clock, where I found Mr. Nisbet's servant waiting to conduct me to his master's house: I ran thither as fast as possible, in order to make my blood circulate more freely, for the cold had been so intense as to freeze my cloaths.

Mr. Nisbet was gone to North Berwick; and his *charming* Lady had prepared for my arrivavl, as if she had boen sensible that I should land near their house.

When Mr. Nisbet returned he could not refrain from personally assisting me to change my dress; when, being quite refreshed, I went down to dinner, and paid my compliments to the *elegant* Mrs. Nisbet. The British women, who fill the higher *ranks of life*, may, I think, be pronounced the *handsomest* in Europe! but the case is different with the *lower class*: this contrast is very striking in Scoltand, where the country girls, and those in servile stations, continually go bare-footed, which practice is also common in our own country; yet the Italian Peasantry, with equal strength, enjoy a far superior *freshness* of *complexion*: the reason of this I take to be that the Scotch Women are often obliged to walk in the wet, their streets and lanes being seldom free from that inconvenience, while ours tread a dryer earth, and for any occasional damp, have wooden shoes.

I conversed with my hospitable landlord most part of the evening: he is a most ingenious gentleman and has resided several years in Italy. Our acquaintance first

first commenced at KELSO; where, while others were dancing, we had a long conversation relative to ROME, NAPLES, &c; though, at that time I entertained the highest opinion of his understanding, yet as I had not then the pleasure of knowing his name, it was some hours before I could recollect where, or when, I had enjoye'd his company; though both his PERSON and MANNER were so strongly impressed on my memory as to appear perfectly familiar.

I arose at nine the next morning and went to breakfast: after which Mr. NISBET obliged me with a sight of his GARDEN, which may *rival* the *most elegant* in ITALY: though now the depth of winter the well stored HOT-HOUSES bloomed with all the beauties of *contrasted* SEASONS, and of *various* CLIMES: but in the summer, when spring has poured out his vast profusion and the simple CHARMS of NATURE aid, and are aided by the ELEGANCIES of ART, what a TERRESTRIAL PARADISE must this be! I shall be strongly tempted to pay it a visit; and, with the friendly hospitable owner, stroll through these regions of pleasure.

> These haunts where the MUSES delighted might rove,
> And NATURE, all lovely, would teach us to love;
> Where blasts from the North might forget to be rude;
> And care on our joys should not dare to intrude.

At twelve o'clock Sir DAVID KINLOCK, with his son and daughter, accompanied by MAJOR MACKAY, came and invited me to his house; where I spent a very happy afternoon, and, in the morning, set off, with MAJOR MACKAY, for EDINBURGH, where I found the generous inhabitants had opened a subscription on to enable me to make another Balloon: but, as I am confident mine will be found, I propose, with the most grateful thanks, to decline this obligation; those already conferred upon me are sufficient to lay a weight upon the feeling heart.

Before *my* arrival in SCOTLAND several attempts had been made to launch a large FIRE BALLOON, but all without success. The poor man who should have gone up, how I commiserate his situation! Judge of his sensibility and misfortunes by the enclosed papers. Do not wrong me so much as to suppose that I have been contented with sitting down idly to drop the unavailing tear over them. I have seen the man; I have offered the voice of consolation to aleviate his distresses; and dictates of humanity have been obeyed as far as lay in my power: alas how circumscribed that power! it is only upon occasions like these that I lament its narrow bounds. Adieu! approve, and join, the prayer, that the UNFORTUNATE may ever find a sympathizing friend in

Your cordially affectionate

VINCENT LUNARDI.

TO

Mr. LUNARDI,

ON HIS

SUCCESSFUL AERIAL VOYAGES

FROM

EDINBURGH, KELSO, AND GLASGOW.

BY J. TYTLER.

ETHERIAL Trav'ller, welcome from the skies!
Welcome to earth, to feast our longing eyes!
Once more we, trembling, for thine absence mourn'd;
Once more we bless thee from high Heav'n return'd.
BODOTRIA greets thee from his utmost bounds,
From GLOTTA's banks incessant praise resounds;
The winding AVON views thee in the sky,
T' enhance thy fame the tinkling murmurs fly.
Applauses loud the lofty forests fill;
Admiring echoes ring from hill to hill.
With gen'rous warmth each honest bosom glows,
Each honest heart, exulting, praise bestows.
Fair TWEED beholds thee gliding o'er his plains;
Thy name resounds from all his tuneful swains;
Thy rising honours Fame's loud trumpet spreads
Where Grampian mountains rear their lofty heads;

Beyond the space of old distain'd with gore,
Where dreadful ROME her arms unconquer'd bore;
Where, mourning, o'er th' ensanguin'd slippery field,
Sad SCOTIA wept her bravest heroes kill'd.
Ev'n frozen THULE shall thy fame proclaim,
From all her barren rocks resound thy name!

 But say, what Pow'r, O fav'rite of the sky,
(Tho' on etherial pinions taught to fly),
To thy bold breast such dauntless courage gave,
When far below appear'd the wat'ry grave;
When tow'ring thro' vast heaven's tremendous height,
The Sea's grim horrors first appall'd thy sight;
When slow descending from the distant skies
The boundless Ocean claim'd thee for his prize?
Or who could guide thee o'er the vast profound,
Where blust'ring winds from dashing waves resound,
Untouch'd, unhurt, again to earth restore,
And safely lead thee to glad SCOTIA's shore?
'Twas HE whose Pow'r the stormy clouds can bind,
Who guides the tempest and directs the wind;
'Twas HE who led thee thro' the tractless air,
And, though thou saw'st not, HE was surely there.
Th' aerial stream sent by HIS high command
Restor'd thee safely to the joyful land.
Superior praise to thee HIS pow'r consign'd,
On thee bestow'd thy matchless strength of mind;
To distant ages gave thy deathless fame;
To future bards he gave LUNARDI's name.

 But how shall I to sing thy praise aspire?
What Muse shall fill me with poetic fire?
Shall I address the fabled pow'rs above,
And boast that Phœbus will my vows approve?
No, let me to some distant region fly,
If such there be, beneath another sky;

Go, court the horrors of wild ZEMBLA's coaſt,
Or, in the dark Cimmerian Regions loſt,
In abject exile hide my wretched head,
Or fly for refuge to the ſilent dead!
On me, alas! the adverſe heav'n's have lowr'd,
Relentleſs fortune hath her vengeance pour'd;
Scarce rais'd from earth, and but to ſink more low,
And more ſevere to feel the fatal blow,
The WHIRLWIND, or black EURUS ſtops my way,
Or angry ZEPHYRUS commands my ſtay;
CONFUSION, DISCORD, all my ways oppoſe,
And *friends* miſguided prove my greateſt foes.

Yet tho' I mourn my fav'rite wiſhes croſt,
My hopes, by FORTUNE or MISCONDUCT loſt,
My conſtant mind o'er each miſchance prevails,
My feeble pow'r yet adverſe fate aſſails;
Once more I try on wings of wind to riſe,
Like you to ride in triumph through the ſkies;
I try in vain;—the bellowing thunder roars,
The gath'ring tempeſt ſcowls along the ſhores;
Fierce NOTUS urges on his furious courſe,
And ſweeps along with unreſiſtleſs force.
Loſt are my wiſhes, loſt is all my care,
And all my projects flutter in the air *.

Proſcrib'd,

---

* To underſtand theſe lines relating to my own misfortunes, it is neceſſary to give a ſhort hiſtory of the Edinburgh Fire Balloon. The machine, from its ſize, was certainly capable of performing every thing expected from it, provided a ſheltered place for raiſing it could have been obtained, and a proper degree of heat applied. The former, however, could not be had. The place, where it was firſt raiſed, was expoſed to the weſt wind; which blew ſo ſtrongly during the firſt week of Auguſt, (the week of the Leith Races), that it could not be inflated until the Friday evening, when the Gallery took fire, and ſome of the Chains ſuſpending the Stove broke, which prevented any further attempt at that time. An interval of calm intervened on the Saturday evening,

Proscrib'd, dispis'd, ah, whither shall I turn?
In silent solitude for ever mourn?
Or shall my hand, urg'd on by black despair,
In monst'rous guilt at once efface my care?

With which was made use of to inflate the Balloon. The Gallery was in little better condition than the preceding evening; nevertheless I was about to step into it, when a sudden gust of whirlwind, common in this Country in unsettled showery weather, expelled the rarefied air out of the Balloon, and otherwise so much damaged it, that no farther attempts could be made that night. By continual pulling and tearing about, attempting to inflate it when it was evidently impossible, and other injudicious proceedings, (for which I do not think myself accountable, because I was not at liberty,) the paper with which the Balloon was lined had been so much damaged, that I now thought proper to take it out altogether, and cover the cloth with some kind of varnish, which might be less apt to receive damage from rough usage. This was done, but as a proper composition could not be afforded, the Balloon, though capable of making one or two experiments, was yet far from being able to endure the fatigue it had to undergo. There was now no Gallery, and the Stove with which it was to be heated, being very little short of 300 pounds weight, was incapable of being taken up, or at any rate without a Gallery, no Stove could be taken. I now came to the resolution of suffering myself to be projected into the air by inflating the Balloon to the utmost, and being appended to it without any furnace, like a log or piece of ballast. You will easily see that this was the resolution of a *madman*, and which nothing but my desperate situation could excuse. A fire balloon in this situation is a mere projectile, and must undoubtedly come to the ground with the same velocity that it ascends from it, unless the person has a considerable quantity of ballast to break his fall as he descends, by throwing it out. Of this it were easy to give a demonstration if necessary, but it is not worth while, as you, will at first perceive it to be true. Having therefore obtained one fine and favourable morning, the Balloon, new varnished, and very tight, was exposed to a very strong heat for near an hour. It was inflated to such a degree, that I am persuaded its power of ascension must have been upwards of half a tun, as a number of people could with great difficulty keep it at the ground.

With

With my own blood seal ruin and disgrace,
And brave the great CREATOR to his face?
———Forbid it Heav'n! let FORTUNE rather shed
Her yet remaining vengeance on my head;

A wretched

With this monstrous power I suffered myself to be projected upwards, seated in one of the small baskets in which earthen ware is carried, without ballast, or indeed without thinking of any. The Balloon set off from the ground with the swiftness of an arrow, but could not ascend more than a few feet, when it was stopped by a rope belonging to the mast which held it up during the time of inflation. This broke its force very considerably, and even when freed from this, it flew with such rapidity that several of the spectators, terrified at the unusual sight, endeavoured to drag it downwards till the rope was forced from their hands. Thus my carreer was stopped, and I arose only a very small way, some say 350 feet, others 500. For my own part, I had scarce time to taste the pleasures of an aerial journey, and during the little time I was in the air, I amused myself with looking at the spectators running about in confusion below. My reception from the ground was much more rude than I expected, and though insufficient to *hurt*, was enough to *warn* me to proceed no more in this way. However, by particular desire, I did take another *leap* of the same kind a few days after, but with much more caution; for I would not now suffer the Balloon to be so much inflated, and desired my assistants to break its power as I ascended, that I might only pass over the adjacent trees and houses. Even then the power of the Balloon was very great, so that it overturned five or six people who attempted to stop it; and indeed, from these two experiments, I am induced to believe, that the power of large fire balloons is much greater than is commonly supposed, and that the received theories concerning them are erroneous.

Be this as it will, my character was now somewhat restored, and a new Stove and Gallery constructed, and indeed my future success seemed undoubted to myself. I therefore announced my journey with great confidence on the 29th of September. A continued tract of rainy weather had prevented any experiment till the very day; the Balloon had been removed into a place sheltered from the west wind, which had hitherto been so much my enemy; but now it was attacked from the east with such violence,

A wretched object let me rather ly
To ev'ry miscreant as he passes by;

In-

tence, that it could not be inflated, even though it was attempted till the mast broke, and no farther possibility of attempt remained.

By this disaster all further experiments were prevented till October 11th. I was exceeding anxious to have had *one* private trial made before I exposed myself to public view; but being over-ruled in this, I retired from the Garden with a resolution to do nothing more that day, and indeed I looked upon a private trial to be essentially necessary. About mid-day I received a message to come down to Comely Garden, where, to my surprise, I found more than 1000 people assembled, who anxiously wished me to ascend. It was now no time to remonstrate. A general opinion of my cowardice prevailed; I was forced to give my consent to the making of signals; indeed it was done almost without my knowledge. The event, however, shewed that the greatest hero on earth could not ascend at that time. The Balloon, after being kept in a state of inflation for near two hours, could scarce bear its own weight. Had I been indulged with a private experiment, I would then have seen what was the matter. The stove in short was too small. It had formerly been made by my directions three feet in diameter; and with a stove of this dimension, I had been raised the two times already mentioned, but as that stove was originally far too clumsy, and battered till quite useless, a new one was necessary. My friends, terrified at the idea of my carrying up such a huge furnace along with me, insisted that the new one should be smaller. I could not indeed with absolute certainty say that this was the least which would answer, but from the most accurate experiments and observations I could make *a priori*, I much suspected the consequence of lessening it. With very great persuasion I suffered myself to be overcome, and consented to its being reduced to $2\frac{1}{2}$ feet diameter, and when this was done, it was reduced, without my knowledge to 27 inches; for my eye did not easily guess the difference, and I never suspected that any deceit would be practised upon me. Thus the power of the fire was reduced in the proportion of 573 to 917, so that as the Balloon, of itself weighing 721 lb. arose with a stove of 27 inches diameter, it would, with one of three feet, have carried 433 pounds more, even supposing the power of fire to be only in proportion to the mere square measure of its

surface

In dull OBLIVION let me rather sleep,
As vile, unnotic'd, useless insects creep;

Let

furface, and I have every reason to believe, that it encreases in a much greater proportion; and if we add to all this the bad state in which the Balloon now was, owing to its treatment on September 29, the smoke pervading it at every pore, I have not the least doubt that it would have arisen with all the weight appended to it, which indeed was very considerable, and was within one pound of the above calculation, myself being 140, the stove 170, and gallery 122.

I had now the miserable consolation to perceive, that *I* had been right, and my *advisers* had been wrong in their calculations. Otherwise my situation was miserable beyond description. I was obliged to hear my name called out wherever I went, to bear the insults of every black-guard boy, to hear myself called Cheat, Rascal, Coward and Scoundrel by those who had neither courage, honesty, nor honour. I was proscribed in the newspapers, and pointed out by two of the Edinburgh News-mongers as a public enemy, and the Magistrate called upon to take notice of me, as if he himself had not known his duty sufficiently without their information. All this I bore with patience; I knew that Popular Opinion, founded on ignorance, varied as the wind, and that a single instance of success would be sufficient to turn the tide in my favour. It was still in my power to get a new stove constructed, and as I might now make it of any form I pleased, without interruption from *advisers*, I resolved to err on the safe side, and made it three feet and a half in diameter. There was now no difficulty but from the bad state of the Balloon, which was become like a sieve, and no public experiment could be attemped. A day was set for a private one, but it proved so tempestuous that nothing could be done, and soon after the whole was arrested for damages; the greatest part of which had never been done by the Balloon, or any one belonging to it. A law process ensued, which lasted six months; at the end of which I was cast. However, matters were compromised, and by means of a friend the Balloon was once more set at liberty. I could not immediately make any attempt, by reason of a fever which confined me six weeks. No trial could be made in the former place, and it was difficult to procure another. The summer was spent in languid attempts to repair the Balloon; and at last on the 26th of July an experiment was made. The place where it now was, had a

shelter

Let fierce REPROACH infulting ever wound,
Envenom'd fhafts of malice fly around,
In wretched darknefs be my poor abode,
By men abandon'd, and oppos'd by GOD!

But while in hoplefs exile thus I mourn,
My mind with defp'rate gloomy paffions torn,
I fee thee graceful and majeftic rife,
Mount on the winds, and triumph in the fkies;
Till envious clouds conceal thee from our view,
And eager VISION can no more purfue.
At once AMBITION points to Fame the way,
Diffolving clouds of cold DESPAIR decay;
Celeftial HOPE again her influence fhow'rs,
Again my foul calls forth her latent pow'rs.
To follow thee my inmoft bofom burns,
Tumultuous thoughts poffefs the mind by turns;
Unconquer'd yet, with thee my fancy flies,
My foul afpiring yet explores the fkies.
Impatient now I long the ground to fpurn,
Like THEE to rife, in *fiery* chariot born;
To leave the earth, to leave the clouds behind,
To mount on pinions of the rapid wind;

fhelter only from the fouth and fouth-eaft winds. A fire was applied for four minutes, the wind blowing gently from the eaft. Some thunder was heard at a diftance, and a vehement blaft inftantly followed from the fouth-weft. The Balloon was torn from the hands of thofe who held it, feveral of them overturned, and their lives endangered; the ftove was dafhed in pieces, and the Balloon itfelf very much damaged. Soon after this, I abanoned the fcheme and Edinburgh itfelf in defpair. Such a feries of difafters is almoft unparalleled; but I pay myfelf too high a compliment in fuppofing that Heaven has declared war againft me: the whole are eafily deducible from want of *power* in myfelf, want of *knowledge* in my friends, and the *impatience* of the public in general.

Beyond

Beyond the reach of vulgar ken to soar,
Beyond the space where blust'ring tempests roar,
To see bright Phœbus pour unsullied day,
While thro' wide heav'n he darts his cloudless ray;
To see the splendors of the Moon arise,
And all the glories of the spangled skies.
Not as thro' VAPOUR's medium dull we view,
The clouded concave of Etherial blue;
But as from ÆTNA, or the Alpine Hills,
Th' exalted mind the glorious prospect fills;
Where GALAXY in purest flame appears,
And wond'rous glories clothe the shining stars;
The moons of JOVE, without a tube to view,
And endless beauties of the heav'ns pursue;
See NORTHERN LIGHTS in flashing glory rise,
And paint their colours of a thousand dyes;
To view bright METEORS like the Sun appear,
And stream their glories thro' the empyreal air;
To try the strong Electric ETHER's pow'r,
T' explore the sources of the glad'ning show'r;
Thro' treasures of the direful hail to fly,
And view the dread artillery of the sky;
Laugh at the labours of the sons of care,
And see them move like *atoms* as they are.

Transporting thought! I'll yet with Fate contend,
Nor shall my hope to dire misfortune bend;
Let lying SLANDER trumpet through the crowd,
Accursed HATE proclaim each fault aloud,
DETRACTION, MALICE, and blue ENVY burn,
And each *misfortune* to *misconduct* turn;
My mind unmov'd fair SCIENCE shall pursue;
My hopes, my wishes, ever follow you;
Each error past, EXPERIENCE shall correct,
And careful PRUDENCE every step direct;

Till rais'd from earth, I to the skies aspire,
Conducted safely by devouring fire;
To future ages then consign my name,
And stand thy BROTHER in Records of Fame.

F I N I S.